America will never be destroyed from the outside. If we falter and lose our freedoms, it will be because we destroyed ourselves.

Abraham Lincoln

I believe marriage is between a man and a woman. I am not in favor of gay marriage. But when you start playing around with constitutions, just to prohibit somebody who cares about another person, it just seems to me that's not what America's about. Usually, our constitutions expand liberties, they don't contract them.

Barack Obama

America was not built on fear. America was built on courage, on imagination and an unbeatable determination to do the job at hand.

Harry S Truman

Terrorist attacks can shake the foundations of our biggest buildings, but they cannot touch the foundation of America. These acts shatter steel, but they cannot dent the steel of American resolve.

George W. Bush

Only in America can someone start with nothing and achieve the American Dream. That's the greatness of this country.

Rafael Cruz

Yesterday, December seventh, 1941, a date which will live in infamy, the United States of America was suddenly and deliberately attacked by naval and air forces of the Empire of Japan. We will gain the inevitable triumph, so help us God.

Franklin D. Roosevelt

The real names of our people were destroyed during slavery. The last name of my forefathers was taken from them when they were brought to America and made slaves, and then the name of the slave master was given, which we refuse, we reject that name today and refuse it. I never acknowledge it whatsoever.

Malcolm X

The promise of America is one immigration policy for all who seek to enter our shores, whether they come from Mexico, Haiti or Canada, there must be one set of rules for everybody. We cannot welcome those to come and then try and act as though any culture will not be respected or treated inferior. We cannot look at the Latino community and preach 'one language.' No one gave them an English test before they sent them to Iraq to fight for America.

Al Sharpton

America needs to understand Islam, because this is the one religion that erases from its society the race problem. Throughout my travels in the Muslim world, I have met, talked to, even eaten with people who in America would have been considered 'white,' but the 'white' attitude had been removed from their minds by the religion of Islam.

Malcolm X

I look forward to a great future for America - a future in which our country will match its military strength with our moral restraint, its wealth with our wisdom, its power with our purpose.

John F. Kennedy

America's future will be determined by the home and the school. The child becomes largely what he is taught; hence we must watch what we teach, and how we live.

Jane Addams

By the 1960s, many of us believed that the Civil Rights Movement could eliminate racism in America during our lifetime. But despite significant progress, racism remains.

Bill Cosby

America is the land of the second chance - and when the gates of the prison open, the path ahead should lead to a better life.

George W. Bush

America did not invent human rights. In a very real sense human rights invented America.

Jimmy Carter

America's fighting men and women sacrifice much to ensure that our great nation stays free. We owe a debt of gratitude to the soldiers that have paid the ultimate price for this cause, as well as for those who are blessed enough to return from the battlefield unscathed.

Allen Boyd

History demonstrates that previous military drawdowns invited aggression by our enemies. After World War I, America drew down forces until the U.S. Army had fewer than 100,000 men in uniform. That weakness invited Nazi aggression in Europe and the imperial Japanese attack at Pearl Harbor.

Frank Gaffney

For a lot of people, Superman is and has always been America's hero. He stands for what we believe is the best within us: limitless strength tempered by compassion, that can bear adversity and emerge stronger on the other side. He stands for what we all feel we would like to be able to stand for, when standing is hardest.

J. Michael Straczynski

America and Islam are not exclusive and need not be in competition. Instead, they overlap, and share common principles of justice and progress, tolerance and the dignity of all human beings.

Barack Obama

America's present need is not heroics but healing; not

nostrums but normalcy; not revolution but restoration.

Warren G. Harding

The essence of America - that which really unites us - is not ethnicity, or nationality or religion - it is an idea - and what an idea it is: That you can come from humble circumstances and do great things.

Condoleezza Rice

My dream is of a place and a time where America will once again be seen as the last best hope of earth.

Abraham Lincoln

America preaches integration and practices segregation.

Malcolm X

What's great about this country is that America started the tradition where the richest consumers buy essentially the same things as the poorest. You can be watching TV and see Coca-Cola, and you can know that the President drinks Coke. Liz Taylor drinks Coke, and just think, you can drink Coke, too.

Andy Warhol

Our nation is built upon a history of immigration, dating back to our first pioneers, the Pilgrims. For more than three centuries, we have welcomed generations of immigrants to our melting pot of hyphenated America: British-Americans; Italian-Americans; Irish-Americans; Jewish-Americans; Mexican-Americans; Chinese-Americans; Indian-Americans.

Ami Bera

The action we take and the decisions we make in this decade will have consequences far into this century. If America shows weakness and uncertainty, the world will drift toward tragedy. That will not happen on my watch.

George W. Bush

The only things that the United States has given to the world are skyscrapers, jazz, and cocktails. That is all. And in Cuba, in our America, they make much better cocktails.

Federico Garcia Lorca

In ten years I will become president of the United States Of

America.

Tom DeLonge

The reason was the failure of both Japan and China to understand each other and the inability of America and the European powers to sympathize, without prejudice, with the peoples of East Asia.

Hideki Tojo

In North America, the greatest threat to the Jewish people is not the external force of antisemitism, but the internal forces of apathy, inertia and ignorance of our own heritage.

Michael Steinhardt

As a black person in America, I am twice as likely as a white person to live in an area where air pollution poses the greatest risk to my health. I am five times more likely to live within walking distance of a power plant or chemical facility - which I do.

Majora Carter

Americans... still believe in an America where anything's

possible - they just don't think their leaders do.

Barack Obama

White America is in the minority.

Malcolm X

In America, with all of its evils and faults, you can still reach through the forest and see the sun. But we don't know yet whether that sun is rising or setting for our country.

Dick Gregory

You can be cool and at the same time respect your woman, who will hopefully become your wife, who will hopefully become the mother of your kids. America needs to get back to family values.

Martin Lawrence

This is what America is about when it comes to understanding that it is equal opportunity versus equal achievement. Each and every one of us has the opportunity for greatness in this country.

Allen West

Bill Gates wants people to think he's Edison, when he's really Rockefeller. Referring to Gates as the smartest man in America isn't right... wealth isn't the same thing as intelligence.

Larry Ellison

My people have a country of their own to go to if they choose... Africa... but, this America belongs to them just as much as it does to any of the white race... in some ways even more so, because they gave the sweat of their brow and their blood in slavery so that many parts of America could become prosperous and recognized in the world.

Josephine Baker

Living in New York City, I am reminded by the Statue of Liberty that the United States of America has always welcomed those yearning to breathe free and seek a better life.

Charles B. Rangel

America offers the most amount of people the best opportunity to pursue happiness on the planet. That's why millions of illegal immigrants have poured into the country

- most of them poor. They believe they have a shot to improve themselves economically.

Bill O'Reilly

America's honor, your honor is at stake. Go out and preserve the greatest country in the history of the world.

Rick Santorum

The legacy of the Armenian Genocide is woven into the fabric of America.

Adam Schiff

Diversity of thought and culture and religion and ideas has been the strength of America.

Gary Locke

There are still 500,000 persons afflicted with leprosy in Latin America, so it is still very much present.

Walter Salles

In America, the stories we tell ourselves and we tell each other in fiction have to do with individualism. Every person here is the center of his or her own story. And our job as people and as characters is to find our own motivations and desires, to overcome conflicts and obstacles toward defining ourselves so that we grow and change.

Adam Johnson

I see people who talk about America, and then undermine it by not paying attention to its soul, to its poetry. I see polarization, reductionism and superficiality.

Azar Nafisi

I have no further use for America. I wouldn't go back there if Jesus Christ was President.

Charlie Chaplin

Internationally, President Obama has adopted an appeasement strategy. He believes America's role as leader in the world is a thing of the past. I believe a strong America must - and will - lead the future.

Mitt Romney

My advice to the women of America is to raise more hell and fewer dahlias.

William Allen White

Let us wage a moral and political war against the billionaires and corporate leaders, on Wall Street and elsewhere, whose policies and greed are destroying the middle class of America.

Bernie Sanders

I have been asked this question over and over again: 'Dr. Jeremiah, do you think God is finished with America?' But that is the wrong question. The right question is: 'Is America finished with God?'

David Jeremiah

In Los Angeles all the loose objects in the country were collected, as if America had been tilted and everything that wasn't tightly screwed down had slid into Southern California.

Saul Bellow

I guess I wanted to leave America for awhile. It wasn't that I wanted to become an expatriate, or just never come back, I needed some breathing room. I'd already been translating French poetry, I'd been to Paris once before and liked it very much, and so I just went.

Paul Auster

In America nobody says you have to keep the circumstances somebody else gives you.

Amy Tan

The job creators are members of America's vast middle class and the poor, whose purchases cause businesses to expand and invest.

Robert Reich

One thing that makes me very happy is to see the growing activism among chefs in America. Chefs like Tom Colicchio, Bill Telepan, and Rachel Ray and food writers like Michael Pollan have gone to Congress, indeed sometimes even have testified before Congress, have lent this support to Mrs. Obama's effort to combat childhood obesity.

Jose Andres Puerta

My Latin temper blows up pretty fast, but it goes down just as fast. Maybe that's why you seldom hear of ulcers in Latin America.

Desi Arnaz

There is a Western world. There is America. There is Great Britain and Germany and France and Russia and China and other nations. I doubt that there is one country amongst those I mentioned which has a desire to see Iran, with its fundamentalist, Islamic, extremist government, possessing nuclear weapons.

Ehud Olmert

Is woman a religion? Well, perhaps you will have the chance of judging for yourselves if you go to America. There you will find men treating women with just the same respect formerly accorded only to religious dignitaries or to great nobles.

Lafcadio Hearn

By dismantling the narrow politics of racial identity and selective self-interest, by going beyond 'black' and 'white,' we may construct new values, new institutions and new visions of an America beyond traditional racial categories and racial oppression.

Manning Marable

The peoples of Asia, Africa, and Latin America have common interest and are in the position to support each other in their anti-imperialist and anti-U.S. struggle. As long as Africa and Latin America are not free.

Kim Il-sung

So the America I came to know growing up was filled with all the excitement and possibilities found in living the American dream.

Mia Love

I was really sad after 'The Avengers' when I realized I was not going to have a part in 'Thor 2' or 'Captain America: The Winter Soldier.' But I'm not arguing with my fantastic plane and my really cool car.

Clark Gregg

My grandmother was born in 1900, and she would regale

me with tales I call 'Little House on the Prairie' tales, but they were tales of segregated and racist America growing up in Alabama and Mississippi, where she came from.

David Alan Grier

And this President wakes up every morning, looks out across America and is proud to announce, 'It could be worse.' It could be worse? Is that what it means to be an American? It could be worse? Of course not. What defines us as Americans is our unwavering conviction that we know it must be better.

Mitt Romney

A citizen of America will cross the ocean to fight for democracy, but won't cross the street to vote in a national election.

Bill Vaughan

Agriculture was the first manufacturing industry in America and represents the best of all of us.

Zack Wamp

Other countries have been founded by 'accidents of force.' America is a creation of thought.

Dinesh D'Souza

I have been so great in boxing they had to create an image like Rocky, a white image on the screen, to counteract my image in the ring. America has to have its white images, no matter where it gets them. Jesus, Wonder Woman, Tarzan and Rocky.

Muhammad Ali

America's health care system is neither healthy, caring, nor a system.

Walter Cronkite

The New Deal is plainly an attempt to achieve a working socialism and avert a social collapse in America; it is extraordinarily parallel to the successive 'policies' and 'Plans' of the Russian experiment. Americans shirk the word 'socialism', but what else can one call it?

H. G. Wells

In America everybody is of the opinion that he has no social superiors, since all men are equal, but he does not admit that he has no social inferiors, for, from the time of Jefferson onward, the doctrine that all men are equal applies only upwards, not downwards.

Bertrand Russell

America is not perfect. It took a bloody civil war to free over 4 million African Americans who lived enslaved. It took another hundred years after that before they achieved full equality under the law.

Marco Rubio

Captain Cook discovered Australia looking for the Terra Incognita. Christopher Columbus thought he was finding India but discovered America. History is full of events that happened because of an imaginary tale.

Umberto Eco

A national legal organization is giving very serious thought to using The Betrayal of America as a legal basis for asking the House Judiciary Committee to institute impeachment proceedings against these five justices.

Vincent Bugliosi

With our technology, with objects, literally three people in a garage can blow away what 200 people at Microsoft can do. Literally can blow it away. Corporate America has a need that is so huge and can save them so much money, or make them so much money, or cost them so much money if they miss it, that they are going to fuel the object revolution.

Steve Jobs

Since belief determines behavior, doesn't it make sense that we should be teaching ethical, moral values in every home and in every school in America?

Zig Ziglar

In Europe first and now in America, elected men have taken it upon themselves to indebt their people to create an atmosphere of dependency. And why? For their own selfish need to increase their own personal power.

Pope Francis

On September 11 2001, America felt its vulnerability even to threats that gather on the other side of the Earth. We resolved then, and we are resolved today, to confront every threat from any source that could bring sudden terror and suffering to America.

George W. Bush

For the first time ever, overweight people outnumber average people in America. Doesn't that make overweight the average then? Last month you were fat, now you're average - hey, let's get a pizza!

Jay Leno

I went through a lot of bullying early on. Girls made my life a living hell. We had come to America from a different country. My brother and I had accents. It was very tough.

Nicki Minaj

America is false to the past, false to the present, and solemnly binds herself to be false to the future.

Frederick Douglass

And by the way, a piece of news, Israel is the one country in which everyone is pro-American, opposition and coalition alike. And I represent the entire people of Israel who say, 'Thank you, America." And we're friends of America, and we're the only reliable allies of America in the Middle East.

Benjamin Netanyahu

Television brought the brutality of war into the comfort of the living room. Vietnam was lost in the living rooms of America - not on the battlefields of Vietnam.

Marshall McLuhan

Oh yes, there's lots of great food in America. But the fast food is about as destructive and evil as it gets. It celebrates a mentality of sloth, convenience, and a cheerful embrace of food we know is hurting us.

Anthony Bourdain

Hurricane Katrina overwhelmed levees and exploded the conventional wisdom about a shared American prosperity, exposing a group of people so poor they didn't have $50 for a bus ticket out of town. If we want to learn something from this disaster, the lesson ought to be: America's poor deserve better than this.

Michael Eric Dyson

It's the movies that have really been running things in America ever since they were invented. They show you what to do, how to do it, when to do it, how to feel about it, and how to look how you feel about it.

Andy Warhol

As you know, I'm an immigrant. I came over here as an immigrant, and what gave me the opportunities, what made me to be here today, is the open arms of Americans. I have been received. I have been adopted by America.

Arnold Schwarzenegger

We must not allow the liberals to move us away from the conservative values of the American past which sustain our present and shall secure our future. As for me and my family, we will serve God, we will serve this constitutional republic, we will serve America.

Allen West

The message is pretty clear: Americans are sick and tired of the doubletalk coming out of Washington, of us going home and saying we're conservative and then coming up here and voting for 10,000 earmarks. We can't fool

America anymore; the media is too good. They're reporting what we're really doing.

Jim DeMint

What's right about America is that although we have a mess of problems, we have great capacity - intellect and resources - to do some thing about them.

Henry Ford

And the American people are the greatest people in the world. What makes America the greatest nation in the world is the heart of the American people: hardworking, innovative, risk-taking, God- loving, family-oriented American people.

Mitt Romney

Football combines the two worst things about America: it is violence punctuated by committee meetings.

George Will

The American dream is dead for the majority of America.

Suze Orman

A black agenda is jobs, jobs, jobs, quality education, investment in infrastructure and strong democratic regulation of corporations. The black agenda, at its best, looks at America from the vantage point of the least of these and asks what's best for all.

Cornel West

I chose America as my home because I value freedom and democracy, civil liberties and an open society.

George Soros

Let me say this: I believe closing Guantanamo is in our Nation's national security interest. Guantanamo is used not only by al-Qaida, but also by other nations, governments, and individuals - people good and bad - as a symbol of America's abuse of Muslims, and it is fanning the flames of anti-Americanism around the world.

Dianne Feinstein

The fascists in most Latin American countries tell the people that the reason their wages will not buy as much in the way of goods is because of Yankee imperialism. The fascists in Latin America learn to speak and act like natives.

Henry A. Wallace

I'm the son of a pediatrician, and I do believe that the most important resource we have is our kids. And I think the most important thing for America's future is to invest more in our children.

Ezekiel Emanuel

There's been an incredible censorship in America and throughout the world, but particularly in America where students aren't even allowed to critically think about evolution, the issue of origins; they are not allowed to hear other points of view; they are taught incorrectly about science and taught that evolution is fact.

Ken Ham

A declaration of the independence of America, and the sovereignty of the United STates was drawn by the ingenious and philosophic pen of Thomas Jefferson, Esquire, a delegate from the state of Virginia.

Mercy Otis Warren

The people made worse off by slavery were those who were enslaved. Their descendants would have been worse off today if born in Africa instead of America. Put differently, the terrible fate of their ancestors benefitted them.

Thomas Sowell

When I was 18, I went to the Soviet Union. I kept hearing that America was planning to bomb them - lots of bombs were going to come down on these people. I went there not knowing anything, except that I thought the whole thing was stupid and that I wanted to see who these people were that we were going to bomb.

Alice Walker

America is my country and Paris is my hometown.

Gertrude Stein

I am running for president to help create a better future. A future where everyone who wants a job can find one. Where no senior fears for the security of their retirement. An America where every parent knows that their child will get an education that leads them to a good job and a bright horizon.

Mitt Romney

I won't be happy until we have every boy in America between the ages of six and sixteen wearing a glove and swinging a bat.

Babe Ruth

What the people want is very simple - they want an America as good as its promise.

Barbara Jordan

Whether they are defending the Soviet Union or bleating for Saddam Hussein, liberals are always against America. They are either traitors or idiots, and on the matter of America's self-preservation, the difference is irrelevant.

Ann Coulter

I'm looking forward to the day when America will mature to the point that we are a color-blind society. I'm not so sure that in politics that will ever be reality, because politics has a way of separating us based on skin color.

J. C. Watts

Let a man find himself, in distinction from others, on top of two wheels with a chain - at least in a poor country like Russia - and his vanity begins to swell out like his tires. In America it takes an automobile to produce this effect.

Leon Trotsky

Regardless of the difficulties we may face individually, in our families, in our communities and in our nation, the old adage is still true - you can make excuses or you can make progress, but you cannot make both! The America I know doesn't make excuses.

Mia Love

There'd never been a more advantageous time to be a criminal in America than during the 13 years of Prohibition. At a stroke, the American government closed down the fifth largest industry in the United States - alcohol production - and just handed it to criminals - a pretty remarkable thing to do.

Bill Bryson

I think hip-hop could help rebuild America, once hip-hoppers own hip-hop... We are our own politicians, our own government, we have something to say. We're warriors. Soldiers.

Nas

It's really unfair to working women in America who read celebrity news and think, 'Why can't I lose weight when I've had a baby?' Well, everyone you're reading about has money for a trainer and a chef. That doesn't make it realistic.

Rachel Zoe

I like to bring people together so we don't waste opportunities and resources and keep doing the wrong things when we know better. Corporate America makes great things and things that can hurt us. They have to be part of the solutions. There's nothing to say you don't make a profit by doing good.

Teresa Heinz

There is no question we need an energy policy overhaul in America. A key part of that overhaul must include moving forward aggressively with expanding nuclear energy as a renewable energy source. Storing nuclear waste is an important piece of that effort.

Erik Paulsen

I think I'm one of the most patriotic people that I've ever encountered in America. I consider myself a bedrock patriot. I participate very actively in local politics, because my voice might be worthwhile. I participate in a meaningful way - not by donations; I work at it.

Hunter S. Thompson

America believes in education: the average professor earns more money in a year than a professional athlete earns in a whole week.

Evan Esar

In known history, nobody has had such capacity for altering the universe than the people of the United States of America. And nobody has gone about it in such an aggressive way.

Alan Watts

The trouble with America is that when the dollar only earns 6 percent over here, then it gets restless and goes overseas to get 100 percent. Then the flag follows the dollar and the soldiers follow the flag.

Smedley Butler

America's health care system is in crisis precisely because we systematically neglect wellness and prevention.

Tom Harkin

Most of all, I dislike this idea nowadays that if you're a black person in America, then you must be called African-American. Listen, I've visited Africa, and I've got news for everyone: I'm not an African.

Whoopi Goldberg

I always see America as really belonging to the Native Americans. Even though I'm American, I still feel like a visitor in my own country.

Nicolas Cage

A tremendous number of people in America work very hard at something that bores them. Even a rich man thinks he has to go down to the office everyday. Not because he likes it but because he can't think of anything else to do.

W. H. Auden

America is the only nation in history which miraculously has gone directly from barbarism to degeneration without the usual interval of civilization.

Georges Clemenceau

Being young and female in America, you watch a lot of T.V., and you grow up on false images of what love truly is. We think the man with the best rap will protect and save us, about it's not usually that way. Then you learn love is something deeper and purer in form.

Lauryn Hill

America is an empire. I hope you know that now. All empires, by definition, are bumbling, shambolic, bullying, bureaucratic affairs, as certain of the rightness of their cause in infancy, as they are corrupted by power in their dotage.

Felix Dennis

To keep farmers on the farm we must maintain a strong farm safety net, but we will also have to build a thriving companion economy to compliment production agriculture in rural America.

Tom Vilsack

The organizers and perpetuators of segregation are as much the enemy of America as any foreign invader.

Bayard Rustin

We have supported state terrorism against the Palestinians and black South Africans, and now we are indignant because the stuff we have done overseas is now brought right back to our own front yards. America's chickens are coming home to roost.

Jeremiah Wright

America... just a nation of two hundred million used car salesmen with all the money we need to buy guns and no qualms about killing anybody else in the world who tries to make us uncomfortable.

Hunter S. Thompson

The fact is, with every friendship you make, and every

bond of trust you establish, you are shaping the image of America projected to the rest of the world. That is so important. So when you study abroad, you're actually helping to make America stronger.

Michelle Obama

If I am elected President of these United States, I will work with all my energy and soul to restore that America, to lift our eyes to a better future. That future is our destiny. That future is out there. It is waiting for us. Our children deserve it, our nation depends upon it, the peace and freedom of the world require it.

Mitt Romney

As individuals and as a nation, we now suffer from social narcissism. The beloved Echo of our ancestors, the virgin America, has been abandoned. We have fallen in love with our own image, with images of our making, which turn out to be images of ourselves.

Daniel J. Boorstin

I went to Zimbabwe. I know how white people feel in America now; relaxed! Cause when I heard the police car I knew they weren't coming after me!

Richard Pryor

This dark diction has become America's addiction.

Kanye West

America's criminal justice system isn't known for rehabilitation. I'm not sure that, as a society, we are even interested in that concept anymore.

Steve Earle

Going back to the moon is not visionary in restoring space leadership for America. Like its Apollo predecessor, it will prove to be a dead end littered with broken spacecraft, broken dreams and broken policies.

Buzz Aldrin

Politics has become infused with narcissism in America.

John Oliver

Let me tell you, it is still morning in America. It just happens to be kind of a head pounding, hung over for four hours in America - and it's shaping up to be a nasty day, but its still morning in America.

Glenn Beck

It's one thing I like about America - they respect the sportsman. They put them up on a pedestal. They don't try to knock them down. And that's a great thing, to be respected by the whole country. It's so patriotic!

David Beckham

We can go back to economic plans that are only designed to benefit the wealthiest among us, like Mitt Romney. Or we can keep moving forward with President Obama's vision for a growing economy that works for middle-class families in North Carolina and all across the country. For me, for North Carolina and for America, it's an easy choice.

Bev Perdue

I'm a promoter of the people for the people and by the people and my magic lies in my people ties. I'm a promoter of America. I'm American people. You know what I mean? So therefore, uh, do not send for who the bell tolls 'cause the bell tolls for thee.

Don King

It took the Gulf War to demonstrate that America did want more than one friend in the Mideast, and also was willing to take and make major risks to prevent a small Muslim country, Kuwait, from being overrun and in effect stolen by Iraq.

Caspar Weinberger

There is no verb for compassion, but you have an adverb for compassion. That's interesting to me. You act compassionately. But then, how to act compassionately if you don't have compassion? That is where you fake. You fake it and make it. This is the mantra of the United States of America.

Dayananda Saraswati

In the 21st century, white America got a wake-up call after 9/11/01. White America and the western world came to realize that people of color had not gone away, faded into the woodwork or just 'disappeared' as the Great White West kept on its merry way of ignoring black concerns.

Jeremiah Wright

I think there's a lot of anesthesia being - that's been pumped into American culture, the mass media television, various forms of entertainment, and the illusion of wealth that we now understand to be an illusion as well as the illusion that America is a world power.

Parker Palmer

No one has been barred on account of his race from fighting or dying for America, there are no white or colored signs on the foxholes or graveyards of battle.

John F. Kennedy

I love being black in America, and especially being black in Hollywood.

Will Smith

Nobody should teach the black man in America to turn the other cheek, unless someone is teaching the white man in America to turn the other cheek.

Malcolm X

My parents shared not only an improbable love, they shared an abiding faith in the possibilities of this nation. They would give me an African name, Barack, or blessed, believing that in a tolerant America your name is no barrier to success.

Barack Obama

There is nothing wrong with America that cannot be cured with what is right in America.

William J. Clinton

The mind of America is seized by a fatal dry rot - and it's only a question of time before all that the mind controls will run amuck in a frenzy of stupid, impotent fear.

Hunter S. Thompson

Now, as a nation, we don't promise equal outcomes, but we were founded on the idea everybody should have an equal opportunity to succeed. No matter who you are, what you look like, where you come from, you can make it. That's an essential promise of America. Where you start should not determine where you end up.

Barack Obama

America was established not to create wealth but to realize a vision, to realize an ideal - to discover and maintain liberty among men.

Woodrow Wilson

Jimmy Carter was - he still - he remains to this day America's most ex of ex-presidents. You just can't believe that we elected this doofus. He was a bright enough guy and sort of well-meaning. But he was about as prepared to be president of the United States as your goofy old uncle, you know, the one that memorises baseball statistics.

P. J. O'Rourke

I don't want you to apologize for being rich; I want you to acknowledge that in America, we all should have to pay our fair share.

Stephen King

In America the majority raises formidable barriers around the liberty of opinion; within these barriers an author may write what he pleases, but woe to him if he goes beyond them.

Alexis de Tocqueville

God has opened many doors of opportunity throughout my lifetime, but I believe the greatest of those doors was allowing me to be born in the United States of America.

Benjamin Carson

Let us build bridges, my friends, build bridges to human dignity across that gulf that separates black America from white America.

Richard M. Nixon

I'm afraid, based on my own experience, that fascism will come to America in the name of national security.

Jim Garrison

In America, the race goes to the loud, the solemn, the hustler. If you think you're a great writer, you must say that you are.

Gore Vidal

America is still mostly xenophobic and racist. That's the nature of America, I think.

Jerry Garcia

In America, through pressure of conformity, there is freedom of choice, but nothing to choose from.

Peter Ustinov

People know something has gone terribly wrong with our government and it has gotten so far off track. But people also know that there is nothing wrong in America that a good old-fashioned election can't fix.

Sarah Palin

America is woven of many strands. I would recognise them and let it so remain. Our fate is to become one, and yet many. This is not prophecy, but description.

Ralph Ellison

Social media has taken over in America to such an extreme that to get my own kids to look back a week in their history is a miracle, let alone 100 years.

Steven Spielberg

It's a great day in America when white people, black people and Latinos can all come together and pick on another minority.

George Lopez

People expected 'Jennifer's Body' to make so much money. But I was doubtful. The movie is about a man-eating, cannibalistic lesbian cheerleader, and that pretty much eliminates middle America. It's obviously a girl-power movie, but it's also about how scary girls are. Girls can be a nightmare.

Megan Fox

I don't believe in quotas. America was founded on a philosophy of individual rights, not group rights.

Clarence Thomas

I do not think white America is committed to granting equality to the American Negro. This is a passionately racist country; it will continue to be so in the foreseeable future.

Susan Sontag

But, actually, it is only Americans who say that our freedoms and prosperity are the reason foreigners hate us. If you ask the foreigners, they make it clear that it's America's bullying foreign policy they detest.

Harry Browne

America was born out of a desire for self-determination, a longing for the human dignity that only independence can bring.

Maurice Saatchi

In the Tea Party narrative, victory at the polls means a new American revolution, one that will 'take our country back' from everyone they disapprove of. But what they don't realize is, there's a catch: This is America, and we have an entrenched oligarchical system in place that insulates us all from any meaningful political change.

Matt Taibbi

We need to tell young people that America was built by men and women of all colors and that the future of this country is dependent on the participation of all of our citizens.

Walter Dean Myers

I've been waiting over 40 years to come to Cyprus, and it has not disappointed - the birthplace of Aphrodite, the Crossroads of Civilization, and, I might add, a genuine strategic partner to the United States of America.

Joe Biden

I honestly don't know, but if America continues to refuse to reduce its greenhouse gas emissions, I see a bleak future not only for American society, but for the world as a whole. This is a global problem that is not going away, and the United States is an obstacle to solving it.

Peter Singer

In America, now, let us - Christian, Jew, Muslim, agnostic, atheist, wiccan, whatever - fight nativism with the same strength and conviction that we fight terrorism. My faith calls on its followers to love one's enemies. A tall order, that - perhaps the tallest of all.

Jon Meacham

It's tough to figure out how do we compete in Europe and North America, when obviously a living wage for us is very different than a living wage in Indonesia.

John Malkovich

The NSA routinely lies in response to congressional inquiries about the scope of surveillance in America.

Edward Snowden

Spending time with America's soldiers is always inspiring.

John Boehner

There's no question that O.J. Simpson had been a substitute white man in America. He had gained honorary white status. He was not viewed by many white Americans as black. He was not seen as the African American athlete who was rebellious: Jim Brown, Muhammad Ali, Hank Aaron... He was accepted in golf clubs that were very tony.

Michael Eric Dyson

The middle of 'America's Women' is about the Civil War, and how women, black and white, confronted slavery and abolition. As in every other period of crisis, the rules of sexual decorum were suspended due to emergency.

Gail Collins

The Obama administration has turned a blind eye to radical Islam since before they came to office. If you look at everything that's transpired since the famous Cairo speech in 2009, it's all been an embrace of those who are the most radical elements in that part of the world. That is not a good sign for America's foreign policy.

Oliver North

You can hear the Celtic heartbeat all over Europe and America, from Bing Crosby to Jack White, from the Smiths to My Bloody Valentine, from House of Pain to Marky Mark and the Funky Bunch.

Rob Sheffield

What we have seen of recent American action in the Pacific, the bombing of Tokyo and the engagements in the Coral Sea, off Midway Island and at Dutch Harbour, has been sufficient indication that America is beginning to discharge her supremely important duty in the Pacific.

Chiang Kai-shek

I love 'Robot Chicken,' 'The Boondocks' and 'America's Funniest Home Videos.' Then there's this show called 'The

First 48.' It's a documentary about killings where they try and find murderers. They interrogate people and they tell on each other - it's hilarious.

ASAP Rocky

For generations, America has served as a beacon of hope and freedom for those outside her borders, and as a land of limitless opportunity for those risking everything to seek a better life. Their talents and contributions have continued to enrich our country.

Spencer Bachus

The brank, or scold's bridle, was unknown in America in its English shape: though from colonial records we learn that scolding women were far too plentiful, and were gagged for that annoying and irritating habit.

Alice Morse Earle

America is a noisy culture, unlike, say, Finland, which values silence. Individualism, dominant in the U.S. and Germany, promotes the direct, fast-paced style of communication associated with extraversion. Collectivistic societies, such as those in East Asia, value privacy and restraint, qualities more characteristic of introverts.

Laurie Helgoe

In America the young are always ready to give to those who are older than themselves the full benefits of their inexperience.

Oscar Wilde

The only foes that threaten America are the enemies at home, and these are ignorance, superstition and incompetence.

Elbert Hubbard

England and America are two countries separated by the same language.

George Bernard Shaw

America is the most grandiose experiment the world has seen, but, I am afraid, it is not going to be a success.

Sigmund Freud

There's not a liberal America and a conservative America -

there's the United States of America.

Barack Obama

Of all the men that have run for president in the twentieth century, only George McGovern truly understood what a monument America could be to the human race.

Hunter S. Thompson

If God doesn't punish America, He'll have to apologize to Sodom and Gomorrah.

Billy Graham

I know of no country in which there is so little independence of mind and real freedom of discussion as in America.

Alexis de Tocqueville

Radical changes in world politics leave America with a heightened responsibility to be, for the world, an example of a genuinely free, democratic, just and humane society.

Pope John Paul II

I'd read up on the history of our country and I'd become fascinated with the story of the Alamo. To me it represented the fight for freedom, not just in America, but in all countries.

John Wayne

There's a love of rhetorical skill in the Muslim world. Osama bin Laden doesn't just go on tape cassettes and say, 'America sucks.' He recites poetry; he finds things that 'America sucks' rhymes with.

P. J. O'Rourke

I think the heartbreak of September 11 - America's grief not only over the loss of life but also the loss of our own innocence - has expanded us as people because it has tenderized our hearts. On a psychological level, the American people have matured as a result of that awful day.

Marianne Williamson

When bright young minds can't afford college, America pays the price.

Arthur Ashe

What charitable 1 percenters can't do is assume responsibility - America's national responsibilities: the care of its sick and its poor, the education of its young, the repair of its failing infrastructure, the repayment of its staggering war debts.

Stephen King

The rivers of America will run with blood filled to their banks before we will submit to them taking the Bible out of our schools.

Billy Sunday

For diplomacy to be effective, words must be credible - and no one can now doubt the word of America.

George W. Bush

America's greatness has been the greatness of a free people who shared certain moral commitments. Freedom without moral commitment is aimless and promptly self-destructive.

John W. Gardner

The founding document of the United States of America acknowledges the Lordship of Jesus Christ because we are a Christian nation.

Pat Robertson

We are a people who do not want to keep much of the past in our heads. It is considered unhealthy in America to remember mistakes, neurotic to think about them, psychotic to dwell on them.

Lillian Hellman

As we look forward to freedom, the shining city on the hill and the best days of America lying ahead, it is the men and women in uniform who protect, defend and make us proud to whom we should look and give thanks every night.

Robin Hayes

It is capitalist America that produced the modern independent woman. Never in history have women had more freedom of choice in regard to dress, behavior, career, and sexual orientation.

Camille Paglia

One of the main reasons America should re-elect President Obama is that he is still committed to cooperation. He appointed Republican Secretaries of Defense, the Army and Transportation. He appointed a Vice President who ran against him in 2008.

William J. Clinton

America is a large friendly dog in a small room. Every time it wags its tail it knocks over a chair.

Arnold J. Toynbee

Breast cancer deaths in America have been declining for more than a decade. Much of that success is due to early detection and better treatments for women. I strongly encourage women to get a mammogram.

Larry Craig

I always liked the idea that America is a big facade. We are all insects crawling across on the shiny hood of a Cadillac. We're all looking at the wrapping. But we won't tear the wrapping to see what lies beneath.

Tom Waits

America is never wholly herself unless she is engaged in high moral principle. We as a people have such a purpose today. It is to make kinder the face of the nation and gentler the face of the world.

George H. W. Bush

You can't have a university without having free speech, even though at times it makes us terribly uncomfortable. If students are not going to hear controversial ideas on college campuses, they're not going to hear them in America. I believe it's part of their education.

Donna Shalala

Candidate Obama promised to fundamentally transform America and that's one promise he has kept. Turning a shining city on a hill into a sinking ship.

Sarah Palin

I know people said I wasn't selling out in America, but that was entirely untrue. We sold out all over the world, and every night I looked out into the fans and those front rows that you're talking about, the tears, the honesty, the inability to not be completely overjoyed because they felt accepted.

Lady Gaga

Black power can be clearly defined for those who do not attach the fears of white America to their questions about it.

Stokely Carmichael

Pakistanis can't trust. They've seen in history that people, particularly politicians, are corrupt. And they're misguided by people in the name of Islam. They're told: 'Malala is not a Muslim, she's not in purdah, she's working for America.'

Malala Yousafzai

In order to lead a country or a company, you've got to get everybody on the same page and you've got to be able to have a vision of where you're going. America can't have a vision of health care for everybody, green economy, regulations - can't have a bunch of piece-meal activities. It's got to have a vision.

Jack Welch

North Korea has taught a great lesson to all the countries in the world, especially the rogue countries of dictatorships or whatever: if you don't want to be invaded by America, get some nuclear weapons.

Michael Moore

America must be the teacher of democracy, not the advertiser of the consumer society. It is unrealistic for the rest of the world to reach the American living standard.

Mikhail Gorbachev

Millions around the world increasingly see America not as a model of democracy but as relying solely on brute force, cobbling coalitions together under the slogan, 'You're either with us or against us.'

Vladimir Putin

Some of the most miserable people I know are some of the richest people in America, they are the most miserable individuals I've ever seen.

Chuck Norris

I'd love to see T'he Avengers' with Robert Downey, Jr. playing Loki and Clark Gregg playing 'Thor' and I play Captain America.

Tom Hiddleston

Postwar America was a very buttoned-up nation. Radio shows were run by censors, Presidents wore hats, ladies wore girdles. We came straight out of the blue - nobody was expecting anything like Martin and Lewis. A sexy guy and a monkey is how some people saw us.

Jerry Lewis

America's veterans and troops serving abroad today fought hard to preserve our red, white and blue, from the Revolutionary War to today's Global War Against Terrorism, and Congress' action today is appropriate for one of our most sacred symbols.

Bill Shuster

Yes, 'Black Girl/White Girl' might be described as a 'coming-of-age' novel, at least for the survivor Genna. It is also intended as a comment on race relations in America more generally: we are 'roommates' with one another, but how well do we know one another?

Joyce Carol Oates

America has believed that in differentiation, not in uniformity, lies the path of progress. It acted on this belief; it has advanced human happiness, and it has prospered.

Louis D. Brandeis

It's almost like a lot of black people in America, a lot of young black men, are born with this cloud over their heads. It's their penitentiary cloud, this philosophy we all have, that it's harder for us.

Erykah Badu

I think Muslims have become the new Negroes in America. They are being mistreated at airports, by the Immigration - everywhere. Islam is a religion of peace. They are wrong.

Jermaine Jackson

We have been terrorised by what happened in America and we express our condolences to the American people who suffered from this unexpected catastrophe and a new world war.

Muammar al-Gaddafi

My biggest concern is that America is drifting towards mediocrity and that people don't recognize - and by people I'm meaning Washington - don't recognize the sense of urgency and the fact that I don't think this is a crisis anymore. I think it's an emergency.

Howard Schultz

Well, if you look at all of the cultures in America, this is a great opportunity for us to really get acquainted with the rest of the world. America is the only place you can do that, but we don't have sense enough to take advantage of that.

Erykah Badu

Get up early and go to the local produce markets. In Latin America and Asia, those are usually great places to find delicious food stalls serving cheap, authentic and fresh specialties.

Anthony Bourdain

Thank God we're not like America. Everyone wants to look like they're 20. In Europe we admire grown-up women; I think men revere older women.

Francesca Annis

Education is the only way forward in Latin America and developing countries in general.

Shakira

In my fight against terrorism, to me, the biggest terrorist is Obama, and the United States of America.

Lupe Fiasco

The economic recession in America wasn't caused by bad luck; it was caused by bad Republican policies. But the Republican candidates are doubling down on the same flawed policies that led to the loss of 3.6 million jobs in the final months of 2008 and gravely affected middle class families across America.

Debbie Wasserman Schultz

At least in America, you have freedom of speech, which is a good thing. It's just a question of whether you're allowed to use it on 'Fox News'.

Eric Idle

This country was founded upon the principle that we are all endowed with certain inalienable rights to Life, Liberty, and the Pursuit of Happiness - those rights are what make America great, and they belong to each and every one of us.

Charles B. Rangel

When President Obama entered the White House, the economy was in a free-fall. The auto industry: on its back. The banks: frozen up. More than three million Americans had already lost their jobs. And America's bravest, our men and women in uniform, were fighting what would soon be the longest wars in our history.

Rahm Emanuel

You know, the diversity that America has is so special. It's starting to really become a cool thing for young people.

Russell Simmons

The great Jewish scientists and philosophers of the last few generations - Spinoza, Einstein, Freud, Robert

Oppenheimer and others - were natives of Europe and America.

David Ben-Gurion

America is God's Crucible, the great Melting-Pot where all the races of Europe are melting and re-forming!

Israel Zangwill

I just got hooked on the radio, the voice of it all. It was my connection to metropolitan America, if you will. Sports, in particularly baseball then 'cause of its rich sediment of numbers, was one of the first things a young person could peg up with adults on - that is, you could know as much about Jimmy Fox as your father did.

George Will

Egypt's problem is that you've got an economy that works for about 40 million people, only you have 90 million people. The answer to the Egyptian problem is not guns, but jobs. We've got to find a private-sector, nongovernmental, aggressive way of creating jobs. That's not America's role totally.

Andrew Young

I decided to make 'Captain America' because I realized I wasn't doing the film because it terrified me. You can't make decisions based on fear.

Chris Evans

It is we the workers who built these palaces and cities here in Spain and in America and everywhere. We, the workers, can build others to take their place. And better ones! We are not in the least afraid of ruins.

Buenaventura Durruti

There's a whole lot of America that looks at each other and says, 'Well, there's 340 million people living in America. Isn't there somebody other than a Bush or a Clinton who can be president in these modern times?'

Jeb Bush

The god most Americans say they believe in is just not interesting enough to deny. Thus the only kind of atheism that counts in America is to call into question the proposition that everyone has a right to life, liberty and the pursuit of happiness.

Stanley Hauerwas

I had been coming to America very frequently for many, many years, so I had plenty of exposure - and maybe the best kind of exposure, because I think first impressions are very important. Maybe I notice stuff that is just subliminal to people who live here all the time.

Lee Child

In America, you have the Cyber Intelligence Sharing and Protection Act. You've got drones now being considered for domestic surveillance. You have the National Security Agency building the world's giantest spy center.

Heather Brooke

Obama ran on a platform of unmitigated optimism - a promise to usher in a brighter day for America. But there could hardly be a greater contrast between his pledge and his performance in office, between his commitment to the nation and his current abandonment of all hope.

David Limbaugh

Out of the agony and travail of economic America the

Committee for Industrial Organization was born.

John L. Lewis

I had no accomplishments except surviving. But that isn't enough in the community where I came from, because everybody was doing it. So I wasn't prepared for America, where everybody is glowing with good teeth and good clothes and food.

Frank McCourt

Going home to Australia, it's good to get home, but it's kind of bad too because you get used to that way of life again and you have to come back to America.

Andrew Bogut

In South America, I heard the 8th Symphony of Beethoven. And the young conductor thought, Beethoven must be heroic. But this is piece which shouldn't be heroic. And this was such a misunderstanding, such a deep misunderstanding.

Kurt Masur

It was wonderful to find America, but it would have been more wonderful to miss it.

Mark Twain

Living in a state of terror was new to many white people in America, but black people have been living in a state of terror in this country for more than 400 years.

Maya Angelou

Perhaps, after all, America never has been discovered. I myself would say that it had merely been detected.

Oscar Wilde

America has tossed its cap over the wall of space.

John F. Kennedy

The world knows that America will never start a war. This generation of Americans has had enough of war and hate... we want to build a world of peace where the weak are secure and the strong are just.

John F. Kennedy

Peace and abstinence from European interferences are our objects, and so will continue while the present order of things in America remain uninterrupted.

Thomas Jefferson

Let us not forget who we are. Drug abuse is a repudiation of everything America is.

Ronald Reagan

Europe was created by history. America was created by philosophy.

Margaret Thatcher

What destroys more self-confidence than any other educational thing in America is being assigned to some remedial math when you get into some college, and then it's not taught very well and you end up with this sense of, 'Hey, I can't really figure those things out.'

Bill Gates

America in its entirety is segregationist and is racist. It's more camouflaged in the north, but it's the same thing.

Malcolm X

America is becoming so educated that ignorance will be a novelty. I will belong to the select few.

Will Rogers

We who follow the Honorable Elijah Muhammad feel that when you try and pass integration laws here in America, forcing white people to pretend that they are accepting black people, what you are doing is making white people act in a hypocritical way.

Malcolm X

I have one yardstick by which I test every major problem - and that yardstick is: Is it good for America?

Dwight D. Eisenhower

America is a nation that conceives many odd inventions for getting somewhere but it can think of nothing to do once it gets there.

Will Rogers

Whatever America hopes to bring to pass in the world must first come to pass in the heart of America.

Dwight D. Eisenhower

I said that America's role would be limited; that we would not put ground troops into Libya; that we would focus our unique capabilities on the front end of the operation, and that we would transfer responsibility to our allies and partners.

Barack Obama

The Negro has been here in America since 1619, a total of 344 years. He is not going anywhere else; this country is his home. He wants to do his part to help make his city, state, and nation a better place for everyone, regardless of color and race.

Medgar Evers

You know if we were to look back and how we were in 1955 living in Jim Crow, living in segregation, living in segregated schools, it's hard to believe that it was America, but it really was.

Anna Deavere Smith

The greatness of America lies not in being more enlightened than any other nation, but rather in her ability to repair her faults.

Alexis de Tocqueville

We women of America tell you that America is not a democracy. Twenty million women are denied the right to vote.

Alice Paul

All great change in America begins at the dinner table.

Ronald Reagan

America's freedom of religion, and freedom from religion, offers every wisdom tradition an opportunity to address our soul-deep needs: Christianity, Judaism, Islam, Buddhism, Hinduism, secular humanism, agnosticism and atheism among others.

Parker Palmer

What people don't understand is this is something that we only have in America. There is no other country in the world where the ordinary citizen can go out and enjoy hunting and fishing. There's no other nation in the world where that happens. And it's very much a part of our heritage.

Norman Schwarzkopf

In the U.S., the '50s and '60s marked the documentary's golden age, especially at CBS, where pioneering television journalist Edward R. Murrow, immortalised in George Clooney's 'Good Night, and Good Luck,' produced such landmark investigations as the CBS Reports programme 'Hunger in America.'

Naomi Wolf

As an immigrant, I chose to live in America because it is one of the freest and most vibrant nations in the world. And as an immigrant, I feel an obligation to speak up for immigration policies that will keep America the most economically robust, creative and freedom-loving nation in the world.

Rupert Murdoch

There is a Providence that protects idiots, drunkards,

children and the United States of America.

Otto von Bismarck

I don't measure America by its achievement but by its potential.

Shirley Chisholm

Babylon is everywhere. You have wrong and you have right. Wrong is what we call Babylon, wrong things. That is what Babylon is to me. I could have born in England, I could have born in America, it make no difference where me born, because there is Babylon everywhere.

Bob Marley

Half a century ago, the amazing courage of Rosa Parks, the visionary leadership of Martin Luther King, and the inspirational actions of the civil rights movement led politicians to write equality into the law and make real the promise of America for all her citizens.

David Cameron

By refocusing our space program on Mars for America's

future, we can restore the sense of wonder and adventure in space exploration that we knew in the summer of 1969. We won the moon race; now it's time for us to live and work on Mars, first on its moons and then on its surface.

Buzz Aldrin

Neutrality is a negative word. It does not express what America ought to feel. We are not trying to keep out of trouble; we are trying to preserve the foundations on which peace may be rebuilt.

Woodrow Wilson

Ignoring fame was my rebellion, in a funny way. I was insistent on being normal and doing normal things. It probably wasn't advisable to go to college in America and room with a complete stranger. And it probably wasn't wise to share a bathroom with eight other people in a coed dorm. Looking back, that was crazy.

Emma Watson

In America today, we are nearer a final triumph over poverty than is any other land.

Herbert Hoover

When the American spirit was in its youth, the language of America was different: Liberty, sir, was the primary object.

Patrick Henry

Where you have the most armed citizens in America, you have the lowest violent crime rate. Where you have the worst gun control, you have the highest crime rate.

Ted Nugent

Everyone in America likely has a bullying story, whether as the victim, bully or as a witness.

Michael M. Honda

America does not go abroad in search of monsters to destroy.

John Quincy Adams

I read in the newspapers they are going to have 30 minutes of intellectual stuff on television every Monday from 7:30 to 8. to educate America. They couldn't educate America if they started at 6:30.

Groucho Marx

Crucial to understanding federalism in modern day America is the concept of mobility, or 'the ability to vote with your feet.' If you don't support the death penalty and citizens packing a pistol - don't come to Texas. If you don't like medicinal marijuana and gay marriage, don't move to California.

Rick Perry

If aliens visit us, the outcome would be much as when Columbus landed in America, which didn't turn out well for the Native Americans.

Stephen Hawking

The things that will destroy America are prosperity-at-any-price, peace-at-any-price, safety-first instead of duty-first, the love of soft living, and the get-rich-quick theory of life.

Theodore Roosevelt

It's never paid to bet against America. We come through things, but its not always a smooth ride.

Warren Buffett

There's a show in America where all these people compete with ferrets, and they don't even do anything. They basically just hold them up, and if they don't bite you, they might win.

Robin Williams

I have only one yardstick by which I test every major problem - and that yardstick is: Is it good for America?

Dwight D. Eisenhower

The glamour of it all! New York! America!

Charlie Chaplin

Anybody intelligent enough to realize what America is, is not going to sit around and do nothing about it. They're going to be the same way that I am. They're going to be the same way our fans are. They're going to be pissed.

Marilyn Manson

No matter the nationality, no matter the religion, no matter the ethnic background, America brings out the best in people.

Arnold Schwarzenegger

Everything I have, my career, my success, my family, I owe to America.

Arnold Schwarzenegger

In Britain, like most of the developed world, stem-cell research is regarded as a great opportunity. America will be left behind if it doesn't change policy.

Stephen Hawking

I was born in Europe... and I've traveled all over the world. I can tell you that there is no place, no country, that is more compassionate, more generous, more accepting, and more welcoming than the United States of America.

Arnold Schwarzenegger

There is not one single police officer in America that I am not afraid of and not one that I would trust to tell the truth or obey the laws they are sworn to uphold. I do not believe they protect me in any way.

Henry Rollins

One of the greatest necessities in America is to discover creative solitude.

Carl Sandburg

All through Latin America, there's sharp condemnation of the criminal atrocities of Sept. 11. But it's qualified by the observation that although these are horrible atrocities, they are not unfamiliar.

Noam Chomsky

In America, sex is an obsession, in other parts of the world it's a fact.

Marlene Dietrich

I wonder what it's like to be from a state that is spread across a few islands way out in the Pacific Ocean, only added to the United States in 1959. Not only that but to be the birthplace of America's first black president? Pretty cool, I bet.

Henry Rollins

One can not be an American by going about saying that one is an American. It is necessary to feel America, like America, love America and then work.

Georgia O'Keeffe

It almost seems that nobody can hate America as much as native Americans. America needs new immigrants to love and cherish it.

Eric Hoffer

True patriotism isn't cheap. It's about taking on a fair share of the burden of keeping America going.

Robert Reich

And let me make this very clear - unlike President Obama, I will not raise taxes on the middle class. As president, I will protect the sanctity of life. I will honor the institution of marriage. And I will guarantee America's first liberty: the freedom of religion.

Mitt Romney

I will begin my presidency with a jobs tour. President Obama began with an apology tour. America, he said, had dictated to other nations. No Mr. President, America has freed other nations from dictators.

Mitt Romney

Since the Revolution, eight generations of America's veterans have established an unbroken commitment to freedom.

Steve Buyer

Whither goest thou, America, in thy shiny car in the night?

Jack Kerouac

When America stopped importing from China, China stopped importing from the rest of the world. This affects Asian countries as well as Australia, Brazil, and other suppliers of raw materials.

Robert Kiyosaki

Although the circumstances of our lives may seem very disengaged, with me standing here as the First Lady of the United States of America and you just getting through school, I want you to know we have very much in common. For nothing in my life ever would have predicted that I would be standing here as the first African-American First Lady.

Michelle Obama

The United States of America will never be intimidated by thugs and assassins. The killers will fail, and the Iraqi people will live in freedom.

George W. Bush

I have never been able to look upon America as young and vital but rather as prematurely old, as a fruit which rotted before it had a chance to ripen.

Henry Miller

I rememeber one time we were getting ready to go to South America and everything was packed up and in the car ready to go and I hid and I was crying because I really did not want to go, I wanted to play. I did not want to go.

Michael Jackson

Every country gets the circus it deserves. Spain gets bullfights. Italy the Church. America Hollywood.

Erica Jong

These old ballparks are like cathedrals in America. We don't have big old Gothic cathedrals like they do in Europe. But we got baseball parks.

Jimmy Buffett

My belief is that guns are too easy to get in America. My belief is that the NRA has bought much of our congress, to the point that guns are actually the only unregulated consumer product in America. Think about that. It's stunning.

Elayne Boosler

It is easier for women to succeed in business, the arts, and politics in America than in Europe.

Hedy Lamarr

America has the best doctors, the best nurses, the best

hospitals, the best medical technology, the best medical breakthrough medicines in the world. There is absolutely no reason we should not have in this country the best health care in the world.

Bill Frist

The most important thing Paris gave me was a perspective on Latin America. It taught me the differences between Latin America and Europe and among the Latin American countries themselves through the Latins I met there.

Gabriel Garcia Marquez

I remember a great America where we made everything. There was a time when the only thing you got from Japan was a really bad cheap transistor radio that some aunt gave you for Christmas.

Cher

Tobacco is America's greatest gift to the world!

David Hockney

It's rural America. It's where I came from. We always refer

to ourselves as real America. Rural America, real America, real, real, America.

Dan Quayle

There are more than 300,000 families in the Gulf region that lost their homes and are waiting for peace of mind. The hurricane exposed the sad reality of poverty in America. We saw, in all its horrific detail, the vulnerabilities of living in inadequate housing and the heartbreak of losing one's home.

Harry Connick, Jr.

What America demands in her black champions is a brilliant, powerful body and a dull, bestial mind.

Eldridge Cleaver

In 1960, when I came out of prison as an ex-convict, I had more freedom under parolee supervision than there's available... in America right now.

Merle Haggard

I wouldn't make an anti-American film. I'm one of the most

pro-American foreigners I know. I love America and Americans.

Michael Caine

My guiltiest pleasure is Harry Stephen Keeler. He may have been the greatest bad writer America has ever produced. Or perhaps the worst great writer. I do not know. There are few faults you can accuse him of that he is not guilty of. But I love him.

Neil Gaiman

September 11 impressed upon us that life is a precious gift. Every life has a purpose. And I think we all have a duty to devote at least a small portion of our daily lives to ensuring that neither America nor the world ever forgets September 11.

Bill Frist

I adore Chicago. It is the pulse of America.

Sarah Bernhardt

America had, for one thing, lived in anarchy for - until

much more recently than Europe. We had the Wild West, where the cliche of the cowboy movies was the nearest sheriff is 90 miles away, and so you had to pack a gun and defend yourself.

Steven Pinker

A serious problem in America is the gap between academe and the mass media, which is our culture. Professors of humanities, with all their leftist fantasies, have little direct knowledge of American life and no impact whatever on public policy.

Camille Paglia

We're not going to have the America that we want until we elect leaders who are going to tell the truth - not most days, but every day.

Ann Richards

Exercise is one of the best ways in preventing the rapid growth of obesity in America.

Lee Haney

The lifeblood of job creation in America is small business, but they can't get access to credit.

Howard Schultz

America is looking for answers. She's looking for a new direction; the world is looking for a light. That light can come from America's great North Star; it can come from Alaska.

Sarah Palin

I mean, the Constitution of this country was written 200 years ago. The house I was living in in Madrid is 350 years old! America is still a project, and you guys are working on it and bringing new things to it every day. That is beautiful to watch.

Antonio Banderas

America's commitment to religious freedom and tolerance should not be conditional.

Mark McKinnon

This year, as we celebrate the 230th anniversary of

America's independence, please remember the symbols that are sacred to this country. Fly Old Glory high and show your respect and admiration for this great nation and the values we hold dear.

Kenny Marchant

In America, we like everyone to know about the good work we're doing anonymously.

Jay Leno

My daddy thought - no, he expected - that my brothers and I and our generation would make the world a better place. He was correct in his belief because he had lived in an America of continual social progress, depression followed by prosperity, segregation by integration, and so on.

Wynton Marsalis

America is the spirit of human exploration distilled.

Elon Musk

'Good Morning America' exploited Joan Lunden's pregnancy, but you won't see me bringing my babies on the air. The only reason I'm talking about the babies at all is that they've been with me on the show since I became pregnant. After a while, I had to acknowledge this pumpkin tummy.

Jane Pauley

America is a hurricane, and the only people who do not hear the sound are those fortunate if incredibly stupid and smug White Protestants who live in the center, in the serene eye of the big wind.

Norman Mailer

We have to fulfill what the real meaning of the Second Amendment is: reasonable access to guns for self-protection and for hunting. And there's no room in America for these semiautomatic, automatic and other kinds of weapons that are simply designed to cause mass havoc.

Alan Dershowitz

And freedom is what America means to the world.

Audie Murphy

In 1945, the world was in a shambles. American companies had no competition. So nobody really thought much about quality. Why should they? The world bought everything America produced. It was a prescription for disaster.

W. Edwards Deming

September 11th was a moment when America had the sympathy of the world.

Tom Ford

Sociologists well understand that chaos at home causes violent behavior, educational failure and social alienation among children. Yet, many of us in America stay far, far away from this topic. That in itself is a national scandal. Bad parenting is gravely harming this nation.

Bill O'Reilly

If I was to say what I am, I'd be a Labour man. I like Tony Blair a lot, I think he's a good man. And in America I'd definitely be a Democrat; I'd never be a Republican.

Elton John

I believe that freedom of speech and freedom of religion go hand-in-hand in America.

Kirk Cameron

America is built around this premise that you can do it, and there are an awful lot of people who are unlikely to have done it who did.

Michael Bloomberg

If I were in politics, and if you ever get me in the White House, trust me, there's a big change coming. What happened to America? We lost our roots.

Phil Robertson

We didn't start this war - the right wing did. We're tired of seeing good-paying jobs shipped overseas. This fight is about the economy, it's about jobs and it's about rebuilding America.

James P. Hoffa

The best way to begin genuine bipartisanship to make America stronger is to work together on the real crises facing our country, not to manufacture an artificial crisis to serve a special interest agenda out of touch with the needs of Americans.

John F. Kerry

America owes most of its social prejudices to the exaggerated religious opinions of the different sects which were so instrumental in establishing the colonies.

James F. Cooper

Globalization and the neoliberal economic model have already been rejected in Latin America; it simply hasn't been a solution for our people. At the same time, Latin countries like Venezuela and Argentina are anti-imperialist and anti-globalization, and yet their economies are growing again.

Evo Morales

I came to America, and I made good. It's an old story, but it hasn't been told in a long time. Usually, it's, 'I'm an immigrant, I came here and got persecuted.' My story is I came here, I worked hard, and it worked out all right. So it's still available.

Craig Ferguson

In America the biggest is the best.

Roy Lichtenstein

The sum and substance of female education in America, as in England, is training women to consider marriage as the sole object in life, and to pretend that they do not think so.

Harriet Martineau

Here's the thing: the unit of reverence in Europe is the family, which is why a child born today of unmarried parents in Sweden has a better chance of growing up in a house with both of his parents than a child born to a married couple in America. Here we revere the couple, there they revere the family.

Elizabeth Gilbert

Natural gas is the best transportation fuel. It's better than gasoline or diesel. It's cleaner, it's cheaper, and it's domestic. Natural gas is 97 percent domestic fuel, North America.

T. Boone Pickens

This nation has been through hard times. But those hard times have hardened our resolve. I'm ready to do the difficult work ahead. But I want to do that work with Barack Obama, and not a Tea Party ideologue. We can move America forward, but we can only do it together.

Harry Reid

America is hope. It is compassion. It is excellence. It is valor.

Paul Tsongas

America's liberal arts universities have long been safe zones for leftist thinking, protected ivory towers for the pseudo-elite who earn their livings writing papers nobody reads about gender roles in the poetry of Maya Angelou.

Ben Shapiro

So many people in this country have a dual loyalty. They have loyalty to America, but they also are determined to have their parade up Fifth Avenue once a year... a Cuban parade or a Puerto Rican parade - many other countries. So they really don't forget.

Tom Wolfe

When people say this isn't the America they grew up in, they're right. Nobody gets to grow old in the America they grew up in.

Gail Collins

In America, we have always taken it as an article of faith that we 'battle' cancer; we attack it with knives, we poison it with chemotherapy or we blast it with radiation. If we are fortunate, we 'beat' the cancer. If not, we are posthumously praised for having 'succumbed after a long battle.'

Abraham Verghese

Each year on the anniversary of Martin Luther King Jr.'s birth, America has the opportunity to reflect on our nation's progress towards the realization of his dream.

Adam Schiff

I am actually extremely casual in certain environments. But one of the reasons I like living in London, I like the formality of it, as compared to the formality of America - or informality. I like putting on a suit. I like putting on a tie.

Tom Ford

Pennsylvania is home to some of the hardest-working, toughest, most decent people in America.

Bob Casey, Jr.

Because if you don't have a great workforce, a great higher education system, you're not going to have the next eBay, the next AmGen, the next, you know, Miasole, and not only California but America is going to fall behind a whole new competitive context which is obviously China, India, and other countries.

Meg Whitman

I had this fantasy that in a democracy the government was the population. So I came to America and got a big slap in my face... Americans were not what I thought. I thought I was going to see bastards and I saw nice people, very friendly to me.

Marjane Satrapi

I have no disagreement with President Obama as a human being. In fact, I'll go so far to say one of the things I respect very much is the role model that he has served as a husband and a father. And I think he has been an exemplary husband to his wife and an extraordinary father to his daughters. Frankly, America needs a good role model like that.

Mike Huckabee

In Scotland, I'm just like a lot of other guys, but in America, I'm seen as a very strong, masculine guy.

Gerard Butler

Over the past two years, the Obama Administration and USDA have worked to build a foundation for sustainable economic growth in rural America. At the center of our vision is an effort to increase domestic production and use of renewable energy.

Tom Vilsack

There is nothing in the genius of America more precious today than the spirit of religious and political tolerance in its application to our own people.

Paul Harris

I asked my parents for permission to study in America and they were so sure that I wouldn't get in and get a scholarship that they encouraged me to try. So I applied to Yale and got an excellent scholarship. I then worked for the Boston Consulting Group for six and half years.

Indra Nooyi

After 9/11, many of the most important news outlets in America abdicated their role as a check to power - the journalistic responsibility to challenge the excesses of government - for fear of being seen as unpatriotic and punished in the market during a period of heightened nationalism.

Edward Snowden

Oceans are one of the most important things in the world now and that is a national security threat of the United States of America, to be honest with you. That is why seeing the habitat destroyed is so short-sighted by us.

Ian Somerhalder

God bless America - what other civilization would give Patrick Dempsey another shot to rule as a sex symbol, twenty years after 'Meatballs III: Summer Job?' His reign as Dr. McDreamy on 'Grey's Anatomy' is proof that there's nothing we love more than giving Eighties celebs a heartwarming second stab at life.

Rob Sheffield

There was a period of time in America where the advertising world actually went to the housewives of America and had them write jingles that would appeal to them. It was actually brilliant marketing.

Julianne Moore

I remember I was a little girl when Elizabeth Taylor stole Eddie Fisher from America's Sweetheart, Debbie Reynolds, and the reaction back then was enormous! And Angelina Jolie was in trouble, too, for taking a husband away from another America's Sweetheart. Don't take husbands from America's Sweethearts.

Jacki Weaver

In America it's live by the sword of freedom of expression and be will to die by it as well.

Vince McMahon

Food is a big part of my culture, so everyone knows how to cook. When I came to America and asked a babysitter to softboil an egg for my son and she didn't know how, I was shocked.

Isabella Rossellini

I think that every minority in the United States of America knows everything about the dominant culture. From the time you can think, you are bombarded with images from TV, film, magazines, newspapers.

Spike Lee

All comparisons between America's current place in the world and anything legitimately called an empire in the past reveal ignorance and confusion about any reasonable meaning of the concept empire, especially the comparison with the Roman Empire.

Donald Kagan

You'd think if anyone could charm America into caring about the evening news, it would be Katie Couric, the Tri Delt from Virginia who became America's sweetheart on the 'Today' show. But her ratings have been dismal - she comes in last place every week.

Rob Sheffield

When you see the misogyny of hip-hop, it's so horrible, it's so putrid, it's so, you know, odious, that we know, we smell, we see it. The misogyny that is reified, that is reinforced, that is subtly reproduced in corporate America or in church life or in synagogues and temples and the like, is sometimes more subtly dealt with.

Michael Eric Dyson

America's support for human rights and democracy is our noblest export to the world.

William Bennett

I think Amsterdam is to Holland what New York is to America in a sense. It's a metropolis, so it's representative of Holland, but only a part of it - you know, it's more extreme, there's more happening, it's more liberal and more daring than the countryside in Holland is.

Anton Corbijn

Generosity has built America. When we fail to invest in children, we have to pay the cost.

Bob Keeshan

In America, we're kind of lazy. But in New York, it's one of those places where you see the majority of people hustling. If you can make it in New York, you can make it anywhere.

Kid Cudi

Natural gas is great for America in so many ways.

Ed Rendell

There has not been a war in South America for fifty years, and I have every confidence that the countries of Central and South America are deeply in earnest in the maintenance of peace.

Frank B. Kellogg

It was the Michael Jordan/Nike phenomenon that really let people see that athletes were OK, and black athletes were OK. Defying a previous wisdom - not only that black athletes wouldn't sell in white America, but that the NBA as a predominantly black sport could not sell in white America.

David Stern

We're the only species who follow unstable leaders. This is true - it has little to do with America - around the world, pack leaders are unstable. Animals don't follow that.

Cesar Millan

Who wants to shake the hand of the first man to put it to America's sweetheart.

John Agar

America gave the world the notion of the melting pot - an alchemical cooking device wherein diverse ethnic and religious groups voluntarily mix together, producing a new, American identity. And while critics may argue that the melting pot is a national myth, it has tenaciously informed the America's collective imagination.

Ivan Krastev

You know, Hoosiers recognize pork when we see it. And they recognize what bailing out every failing business in America means - We're burying generations under a mountain range of debt.

Mike Pence

It was very much like Norman Rockwell: small town America. We walked to school or rode our bikes, stopped at the penny candy store on the way home from school, skated on the pond.

Dorothy Hamill

The argument that somehow we've got to get rid of minority scholarships so that we can have a free and fair America implies that we have a colorblind society where minorities are equal in their pursuit of funds to go to school.

William H. Gray

At every election, my vote goes to the candidate less likely to declare war. You're dropping hugely expensive pieces of exploding metal on a population. America deserves the president it gets, whether the country votes for them or allows their vote to be stolen, and the least we can do is to elect someone who won't do that to other people.

Ian MacKaye

To me, one of the best faces America has ever projected is the face of a Peace Corps volunteer. That face symbolizes this country: young, curious, brimming with idealism and hope - and a real, honest compassion.

Teresa Heinz

I'm an immigrant kid who came to America from India when I was very young and grew up in New York City with a single mom and really was influenced by all of those immigrant cultures bumping up against each other.

Padma Lakshmi

It's time to pull the bandage off America's foreclosure problem. The economy is ready to emerge from its recent dark period, but to make it happen soon we need to speed the resolution of millions of troubled home loans. Six years have passed since the crisis began, yet instead of accelerating, foreclosures have slowed.

Mark Zandi

I imagine an America that can actually change. That we become a nation that prospers again but without pillaging the resources of nations that make their people hate us. That we become a nation that, as the constitution says in its preamble, its very first paragraph, 'promotes the general welfare' of its people.

Richard Schiff

Looking at America's history, ordinary people did something extraordinary. Leaders risked their lives for freedoms that we take for granted today.That's what instills confidence. That's us. We will move forward and prosper because that's who we are as Americans.

Scott Walker

When you say 'comic book' in America, people think of Mickey Mouse, and Archie. It has a connotation of juvenile.

Mark Hamill

The passage of the Civil Rights Act of 1964 represented precisely such a hope - that America had learned from its past and acted to secure a better tomorrow.

Aberjhani

I'd have no trouble being the barbecue kingpin of America. I'd just add it to all the other things I am: jazz musician, carpenter, architect, engineer and revolutionary.

Bobby Seale

Just to have the opportunity to play an American in America is a dream come true for me.

Andrew Lincoln

The great thing about American women is their energy and the way they love to dress. French women don't really dress; they are too conservative, as it's always a question of money. In America, women are powerful and strong, determined. If they want to be an object, they choose to be in control.

Jean Paul Gaultier

After Apollo 17, America stopped looking towards the next horizon. The United States had become a space-faring nation, but threw it away. We have sacrificed space exploration for space exploitation, which is interesting but scarcely visionary.

Eugene Cernan

Although every step must be taken to protect against a chemical or biological attack in America, our nation would survive the use of those weapons as we did when anthrax was mailed to our Capitol and other targets.

Adam Schiff

Ever since the 1860s when photographers travelled the American West and brought photographs of scenic wonders back to the people on the East Coast of America we have had a North American tradition of landscape photography used for the environment.

Galen Rowell

Obama was elected in a flourish of promise that many in the African-American community believed would help not only to symbolize African-American progress since the Civil War and Civil Rights Acts but that his presidency would result in doors opening in the halls of power as had never been seen before by black America.

Douglas Wilder

Within the pages of The Betrayal of America I prove that these justices were absolutely up to no good, and they deliberately set out to hand the election to George Bush.

Vincent Bugliosi

Instead of locking people up and throwing away the key, it's important to invest in them and show them another way - show them what they can do, instead of telling them what they can't do. Because by investing in youth, we're investing into the future of this great nation of the United States of America.

Q'orianka Kilcher

I knew I was the second-best tennis player in the state of Florida and No. 8 in the United States of America when I was 12 years old and I couldn't tell you what I was in baseball, but I liked my chances in tennis of getting a scholarship to college.

Jim Courier

In America, for a brief time, people who followed Coltrane were studied and considered important, but it didn't last long. The result is that the kind of music I played in the '60's is completely dismissed in this country as a wrong turn, a suicidal effort.

Archie Shepp

Embryonic stem cell research is legal in America, and nothing in the administration's current policy affects that legality; 400 lines are currently being used to conduct embryonic stem cell research, both in the private sector and by the Federal Government.

Roger Wicker

I was born in Argentina, June 13, 1943. I brought up my parents very well, so they let me come to America to study at Princeton University.

Emilio Ambasz

If America chooses, we can develop our own energy resources and not be pressured into wars in the Middle East. Cheap energy will restore our economy and wither the economies of our adversaries. It will give us the means to help our allies without sending in the Marines. It will give us more than the Obama options of going to war or doing nothing.

Kathleen Troia McFarland

It's a special place, and I believe in the prominence of America, and having America be and continue to be an exceptional place, and making no apologies for America being a superpower.

Ileana Ros-Lehtinen

When Medicare was created for senior citizens and America 's disabled in 1965, about half of a senior's health care spending was on doctors and the other half on hospitals.

Dennis Hastert

We have so many issues with overpopulation and urbanization and site looting. And this isn't just Egypt. This is everywhere in the world, even in America. So we only have a limited amount of time left before many archaeological sites all over the world are destroyed.

Sarah Parcak

Don't think I am not homesick for America. I say 'homesick' advisedly because I am a man with two homes - America, which gave me hospitality for many happy years, and where my daughter was born; and my native England.

Leslie Howard

There's a lot to love about America - freedom, the melting pot of diversity, individualism - all attractive concepts, especially to an introvert. In fact, the introverts were probably the first to feel crowded in England and to daydream about all the space they would find in the New World. Peace! Quiet!

Laurie Helgoe

Slavery is, as an example of what white America has done, a constant reminder of what white America might do.

Derrick Bell

Our systems are all go. At 9:30 Monday morning trading will resume on both markets, and the message will be given to criminals who foisted this on America that they lost.

Richard Grasso

One thing I congratulate everyone on is the great explosion which has occurred in Washington's Black House and the very important scandal which has gripped leaders of America.

Ruhollah Khomeini

America should meet its obligations in the form of Social

Security, Medicare, our ability to pay our military, legally binding legislation that allows unemployment compensation, the judiciary, the federal court system, the federal prison system, all those kinds of things have to be paid for.

Bill Johnson

On education, in order to ensure that America remains a world leader, we must create an educated, skilled workforce in the vital areas of science, math, engineering and information technology. At the same time, we must give every student access to a college degree.

John F. Tierney

If there is a country that has committed unspeakable atrocities in the world, it is the United States of America.

Nelson Mandela

I am mortified to be told that, in the United States of America, the sale of a book can become a subject of inquiry, and of criminal inquiry too.

Thomas Jefferson

In America they really do mythologise people when they die.

Robin Williams

Building a better you is the first step to building a better America.

Zig Ziglar

In America there are two classes of travel - first class, and with children.

Robert Benchley

I cannot understand how the education of this United States of America has been fooled time and time again. Either make it separate but equal or integrate, therefore it will be equal. And it has been separate and unequal.

Bill Cosby

All around the United States of America - in the cities and the counties - our public education is suffering and has been suffering. Cuts, cuts, cuts.

Bill Cosby

America is another name for opportunity.

Ralph Waldo Emerson

An asylum for the sane would be empty in America.

George Bernard Shaw

The only definition by which America's best days are behind it is on a purely relative basis.

Bill Gates

As America celebrates Memorial Day, we pay tribute to those who have given their lives in our nation's wars.

John M. McHugh

America is a mistake, a giant mistake.

Sigmund Freud

America is the first country... that can actually have a

bloodless revolution.

Malcolm X

In America, there's a failure to appreciate Europe's leading role in the world.

Barack Obama

I try to speak my points of view about black America, and how I feel about black men and the role that black men should play in their lives with their children and in their lives with their women.

Will Smith

Patriotism is easy to understand in America. It means looking out for yourself by looking out for your country.

Calvin Coolidge

When we say Afro American, we include everyone in the Western Hemisphere of African descent. South America is America. Central America is America. South America has many people in it of African descent.

Malcolm X

137 years later, Memorial Day remains one of America's most cherished patriotic observances. The spirit of this day has not changed - it remains a day to honor those who died defending our freedom and democracy.

Doc Hastings

Our friends at the Republican convention were more than happy to talk about everything they think is wrong with America, but they didn't have much to say about how they'd make it right. They want your vote, but they don't want you to know their plan.

Barack Obama

My heart aches for America and its deceived people.

Billy Graham

We can choose a future where we export more products and outsource fewer jobs. After a decade that was defined by what we bought and borrowed, we're getting back to basics, and doing what America has always done best: We're making things again.

Barack Obama

Now you have a choice: we can give more tax breaks to corporations that ship jobs overseas, or we can start rewarding companies that open new plants and train new workers and create new jobs here, in the United States of America.

Barack Obama

Let me even say before I even get inaugurated, during the transition we are going to be having meetings all across the country with community organizations so that you have input into the agenda for the next presidency of the United States of America.

Barack Obama

I don't think the Christian Right dominates America in the way some in the media believe they do.

Billy Graham

There are patriots who opposed the war in Iraq and there are patriots who supported the war in Iraq. We are one people, all of us pledging allegiance to the stars and stripes, all of us defending the United States of America.

Barack Obama

The hardest that I've laughed at a movie was probably Team America. I laughed 'til I thought I was just gonna throw up. I almost had to turn it off.

Ron White

I have learned, in my life and work as a sportswriter, that big-time Sports and big-time Politics are not so far apart in America. They are both a means to the same end, which is victory... And why not? Victory is good for you, and don't let anybody tell you different.

Hunter S. Thompson

The war is coming to the streets of America and if you are not keeping and bearing and practicing with your arms then you will be helpless and you will be the victim of evil.

Ted Nugent

America wasn't founded so that we could all be better. America was founded so we could all be anything we damned well pleased.

P. J. O'Rourke

Yes, America is gigantic, but a gigantic mistake.

Sigmund Freud

I like America, just as everybody else does. I love America,
I gotta say that. But America will be judged.

Bob Dylan

America is not nearly done. We're only in the beginning.
Who knows who we will be? Who knows... what color we
will be? It is all something that, maybe, our descendants - if
they survive that long - will see.

Alice Walker

I continue to care for President Obama and for his family. I
think that in many ways they are very courageous people,
and I honor that, because I know what it means to live as a
black person in a racist America.

Alice Walker

October is a fine and dangerous season in America. a wonderful time to begin anything at all. You go to college, and every course in the catalogue looks wonderful.

Thomas Merton

From the world wars of Europe to the jungles of the Far East, from the deserts of the Middle East to the African continent, and even here in our own hemisphere, our veterans have made the world a better place and America the great country we are today.

John Hoeven

I have found out in later years that we were very poor, but the glory of America is that we didn't know it then.

Dwight D. Eisenhower

Many of you are well enough off that the tax cuts may have helped you. We're saying that for America to get back on track, we're probably going to cut that short and not give it to you. We're going to take things away from you on behalf of the common good.

Hillary Clinton

The enlightenment is under threat. So is reason. So is truth. So is science, especially in the schools of America.

Richard Dawkins

In common with all Protestant or Jewish cultures, America was developed on the idea that your word is your bond. Otherwise, the frontier could never have been opened, 'cause it was lawless. A man's word had to mean something.

Orson Welles

Anywhere in Latin America there is a potential threat of the pathology of caudillismo and it has to be guarded against.

Noam Chomsky

Organized crime in America takes in over forty billion dollars a year and spends very little on office supplies.

Woody Allen

Voting is completely important. People in America think democracy is a given. I think of it as an ecosystem, and what gets in the way of it is politicians and apathy.

Henry Rollins

In America, the professor talks to the mechanic. They are in the same category.

Noam Chomsky

Freedom is a right ultimately defended by the sacrifice of America's servicemen and women.

Arnold Schwarzenegger

Democrats hate America being a world power because world power gives power to the nation instead of to Democrats.

P. J. O'Rourke

America gives every appearance of being a nation besotted with trashiness - divorce, illegitimacy, casual Fridays.

P. J. O'Rourke

When I went into 'Fiddler,' I wondered about the response I'd get - the backlash because I'm openly gay. There was none. I toured Canada and America, and not one single review suggested that I played the role gay or that I seemed anything but Tevye.

Harvey Fierstein

I have made the tough decisions, always with an eye toward the bottom line. Perhaps it's time America was run like a business.

Donald Trump

America's grossly unfair tax system won't lead to class war. Or, if it does, the war will be brief.

P. J. O'Rourke

America is not a wily, sneaky nation. We don't think that way. We don't think much at all, thank God.

P. J. O'Rourke

I believe with all my heart that America remains 'the great idea' that inspires the world. It is a privilege to be born here. It is an honor to become a citizen here. It is a gift to raise your family here, to vote here, and to live here.

Arnold Schwarzenegger

America is just downright mean.

Michelle Obama

America was cool with Saddam Hussein when he was killing Iranians.

Henry Rollins

To me, to be a conservative means to conserve the good parts of America and to conserve our Constitution.

Ron Paul

Millions of students now, in all the schools of America, are reading science fiction and especially, thank God, 'The Martian Chronicles.'

Ray Bradbury

We've got to dumb America up again.

Ray Bradbury

Making duplicate copies and computer printouts of things no one wanted even one of in the first place is giving America a new sense of purpose.

Andy Rooney

The former colonies, in Latin America in particular, have a better chance than ever before to overcome centuries of subjugation, violence and foreign intervention, which they have so far survived as dependencies with islands of luxury in a sea of misery.

Noam Chomsky

People are always angry at America. They're absolutely certain that America either caused their problems or is deliberately not fixing their problems. But the anger is always directed at America and never at Americans.

P. J. O'Rourke

In the late Fifties and early Sixties, opposition to state terror and aggression and torture and so on was zero. That was a horrible time: the massive Kennedy terror operation against Cuba, the first attacks on Vietnam in 1962, the imposition of national security states in South America.

Noam Chomsky

The social and physical construction of suburban America really was quite complex. It was a very elaborate system, and clearly a massive social engineering project that has changed U.S. society enormously.

Noam Chomsky

The prevalence of mobile homes does not correspond with the prevalence of poverty, or with much of anything else. All that can be confidently said about America's mobile homes is that they are massed in places where you wouldn't want to be in one. Florida's mobile homes lie athwart the path of hurricanes. Georgia's are in the way of tornadoes.

P. J. O'Rourke

The importance of local governance may not be obvious to an America accustomed to treating city and state downfalls with doses of federal comeuppance. Sometimes there's a reason for that - the Civil War. More often, all reasoning seems absent - No Child Left Behind.

P. J. O'Rourke

The subculture of felons is in great vogue among adolescents. Enron, WorldCom, Tyco, and so forth allow us Republicans to say to America's young people, 'We be thugs.' The GOP may capture the youth vote at last.

P. J. O'Rourke

Latin America has much richer resources. You'd expect it to be far more advanced than East Asia, but it had the disadvantage of being under imperialist wings.

Noam Chomsky

You can't destroy America by destroying our elite. Think about America's elite. Think about it down through history. Destroy our elite, and about half the time, you're doing us a favor.

P. J. O'Rourke

Politics in America is like stale bread. It's so yada yada that the best among us can hardly stand it.

Marianne Williamson

Public schools helped create the idea of America and

inculcate Americans with a few rudiments of knowledge. To judge by that very American item, the Internet, a few rudiments is all anyone cares to have.

P. J. O'Rourke

America is a model of force and freedom and moderation - with all the coarseness and rudeness of its people.

Lord Byron

Seven-11 is the pulse-beat of America. I think that Bruce Springsteen should do a song about a 7-11 in Asbury Park, New Jersey, but write it in such a way that American's youth can identify and slurp along with the Boss. Hail the Boss! Hail 7-11!

Henry Rollins

What's great about this country is that America started the tradition where the richest consumers buy essentially the same things as the poorest.

Andy Warhol

Barack Obama's administration responded to the Haitian

crisis within 24 hours. Here comes the soldiers, here comes the food, go go go... Rush Limbaugh told his multi-millions of listeners that Obama only did that to gain favour with black people in America. This is the kind of idiocy that I have to deal with in my country.

Henry Rollins

I think America is just so in love with conflict.

Chuck Palahniuk

The spirit of America has nurtured responsibility and community unlike any other country.

Stephen Covey

In many ways, America is on the receiving end of a pendulum that has been swung with great force, and for a long time, outward into the world. The impact is a wake-up call on every level.

Henry Rollins

If American forces leave Afghanistan, the Taliban is going to do what to America? Don't say you're worried about what they will do to the Afghan people. If that was America's concern, America's operational presence there would be much different.

Henry Rollins

George Zimmerman is a foot soldier in a rapidly privatizing country. He is a new centurion of 21st-century America. Law enforcement is tied down by the strictures of, well, the law. There is only 'so much they can do' to take care of the 'problem.'

Henry Rollins

It is instilled in thousands of American males from an early age that one of their requirements is to be able to both dish out and take a lot of pain. They are taught the rules of this road in gyms, rings, backyards and fields all over America.

Henry Rollins

The first time probably people really were aware of me, I unfortunately had the title of Showtime's Funniest Person in America. And that's a really tough title to travel around with when you're not even known.

Ellen DeGeneres

America is off-the-hook gay. I will not go all Ann Coulter on you and say, 'Our gays are better than their gays,' but as far as countries go, we are in-your-face gay.

Henry Rollins

America is an enormous frosted cupcake in the middle of millions of starving people.

Gloria Steinem

We're enlarging in every single area of the ministry at In Touch. We're on radio and television. We're in over 110 million homes in America plus radio on satellites. We just acquired the NAMB FamilyNet television network, and with that expanding possibilities of the gospel.

Charles Stanley

I'm not a reality-TV kind of guy. But it's almost like we're living in a reality show. Every day in this country, everybody keeps worrying about the deterioration of America, and it's like a big reality show.

Clint Eastwood

I wish President Obama had succeeded because I want America to succeed. But his promises gave way to disappointment and division. This isn't something we have to accept. Now is the moment when we can do something. With your help we will do something.

Mitt Romney

From 1945 to 1974, the Western world - including America - was more socialistic than capitalistic, more pro-labor than pro-business.

Robert Kiyosaki

The worst thing about Halloween is, of course, candy corn. It's unbelievable to me. Candy corn is the only candy in the history of America that's never been advertised. And there's a reason. All of the candy corn that was ever made was made in 1911. And so, since nobody eats that stuff, every year there's a ton of it left over.

Lewis Black

Everyone assumes America must play the leading role in crafting some settlement or compromise between the Israelis and the Palestinians. But Jefferson, Madison, and

Washington explicitly warned against involving ourselves in foreign conflicts.

Ron Paul

America puts killers on the cover of 'TIME' magazine, giving them as much notoriety as our favorite movie stars.

Marilyn Manson

Tortoises can survive for weeks without food or water, easily long enough to float in the Humboldt Current from South America to the Galapagos Islands.

Richard Dawkins

America took me into her bosom when there was no longer a country worthy of the name, but in my heart I am German - German in my soul.

Marlene Dietrich

Conservatism is not about leaving people behind. Conservatism is about empowering people to catch up, to give them the tools at their disposable that make it possible for them to access all the hope, all the promise, all the opportunity that America offers. And our programs to help them should reflect that.

Marco Rubio

If you're going to America, bring your own food.

Fran Lebowitz

Hopping the fence or wading the Rio Grande River isn't part of America's immigration process.

Ted Nugent

Sex. In America an obsession. In other parts of the world a fact.

Marlene Dietrich

It strikes me as odd that the free exercise of religious faith is sometimes treated as a problem, something America is stuck with instead of blessed with.

Mitt Romney

America will be far safer if we reduce the chances of a terrorist attack in one of our cities than if we diminish the civil liberties of our own people.

Nancy Pelosi

Education is a fundamental principle of what made America a success. We can't afford to throw any young people away.

Benjamin Carson

Eighty percent of married men cheat in America. The rest cheat in Europe.

Jackie Mason

It's heartbreaking that so many hundreds of millions of people around the world are desperate for the right to vote, but here in America people stay home on election day.

Moby

The promise of America has always been that if you worked hard, had the right values, took some risks, that there was an opportunity to build a better life for your family and for your next generation.

Mitt Romney

I do have my ducks in line if I want to do it, but I'd love to see the Republicans pick somebody that was going to win and take over this country and frankly, to use the expression, 'Make America great again.'

Donald Trump

Mr. Chairman, delegates. I accept your nomination for President of the United States of America. I do so with humility, deeply moved by the trust you have placed in me. It is a great honor. It is an even greater responsibility.

Mitt Romney

America, which has the most glorious present still existing in the world today, hardly stops to enjoy it, in her insatiable appetite for the future.

Anne Morrow Lindbergh

And that's how it is in America. We look to our communities, our faiths, our families for our joy, our support, in good times and bad. It is both how we live our lives and why we live our lives.

Mitt Romney

Sons of Islam everywhere, the jihad is a duty - to establish the rule of Allah on earth and to liberate your countries and yourselves from America's domination and its Zionist allies, it is your battle - either victory or martyrdom.

Ahmed Yassin

I always consider the settlement of America with reverence and wonder, as the opening of a grand scene and design in providence, for the illumination of the ignorant and the emancipation of the slavish part of mankind all over the earth.

John Adams

They talk about the failure of socialism but where is the success of capitalism in Africa, Asia and Latin America?

Fidel Castro

Justice is expensive in America. There are no Free Passes...

You might want to remember this, the next time you get careless and blow off a few Parking Tickets. They will come back to haunt you the next time you see a Cop car in your rear-view mirror.

Hunter S. Thompson

Every morning I get up and look through the Forbes list of the richest people in America. If I'm not there, I go to work.

Robert Orben

I ran away from home. I ran away from St. Louis, and then I ran away from the United States of America, because of that terror of discrimination, that horrible beast which paralyzes one's very soul and body.

Josephine Baker

My answer to the racial problem in America is to not deal with it at all. The founding fathers dealt with it when they made the Constitution.

James Meredith

I greatly fear some of America's greatest and most

dangerous enemies are such as think themselves her best friends.

Nathan Hale

We must always remember that America is a great nation today not because of what government did for people but because of what people did for themselves and for one another.

Richard M. Nixon

Ultimately, America's answer to the intolerant man is diversity, the very diversity which our heritage of religious freedom has inspired.

Robert Kennedy

America was born as a nation of immigrants who have always contributed to its greatness.

Charles B. Rangel

We are a nation of immigrants. We are the children and grandchildren and great-grandchildren of the ones who wanted a better life, the driven ones, the ones who woke up at night hearing that voice telling them that life in that place called America could be better.

Mitt Romney

The United Nations' founders understood that decisions affecting war and peace should happen only by consensus, and with America's consent, the veto by Security Council permanent members was enshrined in the United Nations Charter. The profound wisdom of this has underpinned the stability of international relations for decades.

Vladimir Putin

Ours is a country built more on people than on territory. The Jews will come from everywhere: from France, from Russia, from America, from Yemen... Their faith is their passport.

David Ben-Gurion

I live in America. I have the right to write whatever I want. And it's equaled by another right just as powerful: the right not to read it. Freedom of speech includes the freedom to offend people.

Brad Thor

And you have to remember that I came to America as an immigrant. You know, on a ship, through the Statue of Liberty. And I saw that skyline, not just as a representation of steel and concrete and glass, but as really the substance of the American Dream.

Daniel Libeskind

Liquor prohibition led to the rise of organized crime in America, and drug prohibition has led to the rise of the gang problems we have now.

Drew Carey

We Muslims believe that the white race, which is guilty of having oppressed and exploited and enslaved our people here in America, should and will be the victims of God's divine wrath.

Malcolm X

The school is the last expenditure upon which America should be willing to economize.

Franklin D. Roosevelt

In the 1940s, cigarettes would be shown in classy situations, endorsed by celebrities - real A-list Hollywood stars in America - the ads would make claims about tobacco quality or manufacturing science and, bizarrely, some brands had what almost amounted to health claims.

Peter York

Are we simply waving farewell to the days when some of the most interesting thinking in Europe and America came to us from our fiction film-makers? BBC2, which once introduced and showed great films, now shows none.

David Hare

When it comes to idiots, America's got more than its fair share. If idiots were energy, it would be a source that would never run out.

Lewis Black

There is not a liberal America and a conservative America - there is the United States of America. There is not a black America and a white America and latino America and asian America - there's the United States of America.

Barack Obama

Imagine a political system so radical as to promise to move more of the poorest 20% of the population into the richest 20% than remain in the poorest bracket within the decade? You don't need to imagine it. It's called the United States of America.

Thomas Sowell

Mass transportation is doomed to failure in North America because a person's car is the only place where he can be alone and think.

Marshall McLuhan

Central to America's rise to global leadership is our Judeo-Christian tradition with the vision of the goodness and possibilities of every human life.

Mitt Romney

I've met graduating college kids facing loan payments and a bad economy, and they are worried that they won't be able to get a job. This is not the way America needs to be.

Mitt Romney

In America the schools have become too permissive, the kids now are controlling the schools, the tail is wagging the dog. We've got to make a change there and get it back to where the teachers have control of the classrooms.

Chuck Norris

This is the America that I love. This is a great people. We can do anything. We can achieve anything. We've got a government that has gotten in the way of the American people. We're going to change that in November.

Mitt Romney

I see America spreading disaster. I see America as a black curse upon the world. I see a long night settling in and that mushroom which has poisoned the world withering at the roots.

Henry Miller

The America we all know has been a story of the many becoming one, uniting to preserve liberty, uniting to build the greatest economy in the world, uniting to save the world from unspeakable darkness.

Mitt Romney

In America, educators punish those who actually think for themselves. There is only acceptance for popular opinion.

Bryant H. McGill

America will always side with those whom she can direct, give orders to and have those orders obeyed.

Louis Farrakhan

American and Israel share a special bond. Our relationship is unique among all nations. Like America, Israel is a strong democracy, a symbol of freedom, and an oasis of liberty, a home to the oppressed and persecuted.

William J. Clinton

I think Barack Obama is a socialist. I think he cares for his country - don't get me wrong about that - but I think he truly misunderstands what this country was based upon, the values that America was based upon, which was free enterprise and having the ability to risk your capital and having a chance to have a return on your investment.

Rick Perry

I have never been a quitter. To leave office before my term is completed is opposed to every instinct in my body. But as president I must put the interests of America first Therefore, I shall resign the presidency effective at noon tomorrow.

Richard M. Nixon

I will never relent in defending America - whatever it takes.

George W. Bush

Watch the walls come down, whether it's in the South or on Wall Street. When the walls come down, what do we find? More markets, more talent, more capital and growth. Which means that the race and sex discrimination stunt economic growth. It's not good for capitalism. It's not good for America's growth. And it's not morally right.

Jesse Jackson

America is not anything if it consists of each of us. It is

something only if it consists of all of us.

Woodrow Wilson

There is no doubt that America remains the premier political, economic, military power in the world, and I both expect and count on it remaining so, because I think that's certainly in our best interest but also the best interests of the world.

Hillary Clinton

Great tragedy has come to us, and we are meeting it with the best that is in our country, with courage and concern for others because this is America. This is who we are.

George W. Bush

CNN found that Hillary Clinton is the most admired woman in America. Women admire her because she's strong and successful. Men admire her because she allows her husband to cheat and get away with it.

Jay Leno

Our society is illuminated by the spiritual insights of the

Hebrew prophets. America and Israel have a common love of human freedom, and they have a common faith in a democratic way of life.

Lyndon B. Johnson

America lives in the heart of every man everywhere who wishes to find a region where he will be free to work out his destiny as he chooses.

Woodrow Wilson

Hundreds of thousands of American servicemen and women are deployed across the world in the war on terror. By bringing hope to the oppressed, and delivering justice to the violent, they are making America more secure.

George W. Bush

It was so much fun to have the freedom to wander America, with no assignments. For 25 or 30 years I never had an assignment. These were all stories I wanted to do myself.

Charles Kuralt

If you think Independence Day is America's defining

holiday, think again. Thanksgiving deserves that title, hands-down.

Tony Snow

Sometimes people call me an idealist. Well, that is the way I know I am an American. America is the only idealistic nation in the world.

Woodrow Wilson

America must be a light to the world, not just a missile.

Nancy Pelosi

It will be helpful in our mutual objective to allow every man in America to look his neighbor in the face and see a man-not a color.

Adlai E. Stevenson

I may be the only mother in America who knows exactly what their child is up to all the time.

Barbara Bush

The political lesson of Watergate is this: Never again must America allow an arrogant, elite guard of political adolescents to by-pass the regular party organization and dictate the terms of a national election.

Gerald R. Ford

The hope and change the Democrats had in mind was nothing more than a retread of the failed and discredited socialist policies that have been the enemy of freedom for centuries all over the world. I fear America is teetering towards tyranny.

Jim DeMint

I am going to take something I learned over in Israel. Their Independence Day is preceded the 24 hours before with Memorial Day, so it gives them a chance to serve and reflect and then celebrate. I am going to try to start that tradition here in America.

Glenn Beck

Like it or not children are being raised by gay and lesbian parents all over America - as many as 10 million children. And it does nothing to make their lives more stable and secure to attack their families, to attack their parents to prevent us from marrying each other.

Dan Savage

Anarchy may await America, due to the daily injustices suffered by the people.

Louis Farrakhan

In America most everybody who's Italian is half Italian. Except me. I'm all Italian. I'm mostly Sicilian, and I have a little bit of Neapolitan in me. You get your full dose with me.

Al Pacino

President Obama's approach embodies the values, the ideas, and the direction America must take to build a 21st century version of the American Dream in a nation of shared opportunities, shared prosperity and shared responsibilities.

William J. Clinton

Let me tell you who we conservatives are: we love people. When we look out over the United States of America, when we are anywhere, when we see a group of people, such as this or anywhere, we see Americans. We see human beings. We don't see groups. We don't see victims.

Rush Limbaugh

America's strength is not our diversity; our strength is our ability to unite people of different backgrounds around common principles. A common language is necessary to reach that goal.

Ernest Istook

Without an advocate for the poor, without a new state of mind in America, the country lies on the brink of anarchy.

Louis Farrakhan

America's Veterans have served their country with the belief that democracy and freedom are ideals to be upheld around the world.

John Doolittle

The amazing fact is that America is founded on a document. It's a work in progress. It can be tested by each generation.

Christopher Hitchens

Too small is our world to allow discrimination, bigotry and intolerance to thrive in any corner of it, let alone in the United States of America.

Eliot Engel

Discussion in America means dissent.

James Thurber

The biggest difference between England and America is that England has history, while America has geography.

Neil Gaiman

America will nurture a new Muslim - one who can believe in Muhammad and the Quran but who abandons belief in a Shariah-based state and affirms the primary American value of individual liberty, which has not been a normative Islamic value.

Dennis Prager

I have never written that there is a threat of fascism in America. I always considered the idea overwrought. But now I believe there really is such a threat - and it will come draped not in an American flag, but in the name of tolerance and health.

Dennis Prager

With Americans worried about losing their jobs, their savings, their homes and their chance at the American Dream, the New Direction Congress will work in a bipartisan way to lift our economy and help America's middle class.

Nancy Pelosi

The largest party in America, by the way, is neither the Democrats nor the Republicans. It's the party of non-voters.

Robert Reich

America is a vast conspiracy to make you happy.

John Updike

In America we can say what we think, and even if we can't think, we can say it anyhow.

Charles Kettering

America is not just a country, it's an idea, and real Americans are getting busy.

Bono

America is the greatest country in the whole world.

Chris Rock

What we do is as American as lynch mobs. America has always been a complex place.

Jerry Garcia

If I were to live my life over again, I would be an American. I would steep myself in America, I would know no other land.

Henry James

The Supreme Court has insulted you over and over again, Lord. They've taken your Bible away from the schools. They've forbidden little children to pray. They've taken the knowledge of God as best they can, and organizations have come into court to take the knowledge of God out of the public square of America.

Pat Robertson

People in the U.K. share my bemusement with the United States that America doesn't share with itself. They have a sense of irony, which America doesn't have, seeing as it's being run by fundamentalists who take things literally.

Bill Hicks

Stupid people are ruining America.

Herman Cain

When asked by an anthropologist what the Indians called America before the white man came, an Indian said simply, 'Ours.'

Vine Deloria, Jr.

Australians are coffee snobs. An influx of Italian immigrants after World War II ensured that - we probably had the word 'cappuccino' about 20 years before America. Cafe culture is really big for Aussies. We like to work hard, but we take our leisure time seriously.

Hugh Jackman

Everybody in America started to define themselves by all these things they had around them. And all of a sudden it came tumbling down. So the old American dream has died, and that is a good thing.

Suze Orman

America has everything, why should they want us.

George Harrison

No one is more sentimentalized in America than mothers on Mother's Day, but no one is more often blamed for the culture's bad people and behavior.

Anne Lamott

America is the story of everyday people who did extraordinary things. A story woven deep into the fabric of our society.

Marco Rubio

America's veterans embody the ideals upon which America was founded more than 229 years ago.

Steve Buyer

Europe's the mayonnaise, but America supplies the good old lobster.

D. H. Lawrence

But more than anything else, for the British folks Irish people were all terrorists. So when we went to Britain, it was always a lot of resistance to U2. And that's why we came to America.

Bono

America may be the best country in the world, but that's kind of like being the valedictorian of summer school.

Dennis Miller

For 70 nights, right across America, I've been getting out there with two ex-lovers and we've been playing songs which are so specific about each of us, you just wouldn't know. We're friends now but we can't forget what happened between us.

Stevie Nicks

The victim mentality may be the last uncomplicated thing about life in America.

Anna Quindlen

I'm a very shy person, and I never tried to do theater. I've been asked many, many times by the most incredible authors in America to do theater. And I always said no, not knowing what it is to be on the stage and to do theater.

Sophia Loren

Every two years the American politics industry fills the airwaves with the most virulent, scurrilous, wall-to-wall character assassination of nearly every political practitioner in the country - and then declares itself puzzled that America has lost trust in its politicians.

Charles Krauthammer

What is the essence of America? Finding and maintaining that perfect, delicate balance between freedom 'to' and freedom 'from.'

Marilyn vos Savant

As a result of that, America desires a moderate Islam; an Islam that America can control; an Islam that America can give direction to and give orders to its leaders.

Louis Farrakhan

I probably have traveled and walked into more variety stores than anybody in America.

Sam Walton

Yes, this is 21st-century America. Where we have better means to treat mental illness than ever before, but choose to let the insane people decide to get it or not.

Rich Lowry

America is the best half-educated country in the world.

Nicholas M. Butler

America is a land where men govern, but women rule.

John Mason Brown

Teachers have the hardest and most important jobs in America. They're building our nation. And we should appreciate them, respect them, and pay them well.

Jim Hunt

Political debate with liberals is basically impossible in America today because liberals are calling names while conservatives are trying to make arguments.

Ann Coulter

I feel bad for the kids that are in school right now and the young people all across America who don't realize that the grownups who are supposed to be running this country are the verge of leaving them as the first generation of Americans worse off than the generation before.

Marco Rubio

Science is definitely part of America's infrastructure, the engine of prosperity. And yet science is given almost no visibility in the media.

Michio Kaku

I must try and break through the cliches about Latin America. Superpowers and other outsiders have fought over us for centuries in ways that have nothing to do with our problems. In reality we are all alone.

Gabriel Garcia Marquez

Everybody in America is soft, and hates conflict. The cure for this, both in politics and social life, is the same - hardihood. Give them raw truth.

John Jay Chapman

The lesson of 9/11 is that America is truly exceptional. We withstood the worst attack of our history, intended by our enemies to destroy us. Instead, it drew us closer and made us more united. Our love for freedom and one another has given us a strength that surprised even ourselves.

Rudy Giuliani

These terrorists aren't trying to kill us because we offended them. They attack us because they want to impose their view of the world on as many people as they can, and America is standing in their way.

Marco Rubio

I can remember when Democrats believed that it was the duty of America to fight for freedom over tyranny.

Zell Miller

America's a family. We all yell at each other. It all works out.

Louis C. K.

The White House used to be, everybody looked up at the White House and America and everything, and now I think it's like a house of shame.

Jonathan Davis

From secrecy and deception in high places, come home, America. From military spending so wasteful that it weakens our nation, come home, America.

George McGovern

Together we can and must fight for justice for our children and protect them from draconian tax cuts and budget choices that threaten their survival, education and preparation for the future. If they are not ready for tomorrow, neither is America.

Marian Wright Edelman

There are hardly five critics in America; and several of them are asleep.

Herman Melville

We should be the pro-legal immigration party. A party that has a positive platform and agenda on how we can create a legal immigration system that works for immigrants and works for America.

Marco Rubio

I want to be America's Margaret Thatcher. I will be the next Iron Lady.

Michele Bachmann

I have dual citizenship, it just so happens I live in America.

Anthony Hopkins

What is going on in America is extreme. The youth cult, they worship youth so much it's almost paranoid. And LA is the Mecca of it all; they're taking it to the hilt.

Billie Joe Armstrong

Contrary to what those in power would like you to believe so that you'll give up your pension, cut your wages, and settle for the life your great-grandparents had, America is not broke. Not by a long shot. The country is awash in wealth and cash.

Michael Moore

I would give the people of America to their first opportunity to elect a president who doesn't belong to either party since George Washington.

Jesse Ventura

I have dual citizenship; it just so happens I live in America. I would like to go back to Wales. I'm obsessed with my childhood, and at least three times a week dream I am back there.

Anthony Hopkins

Wall Street, the banks, and corporate America, has been able to call the shots here. They control our members of Congress and they get what they want.

Michael Moore

A lot of what is wrong with corporate America has to do with a culture filled with antibodies trained to expel anything different. HR departments often want cookie cutter employees, which inevitably results in cookie cutter solutions.

Nolan Bushnell

Here in England, everyone's a pop star, innit, whereas in America they believe in the term artist.

Amy Winehouse

Baseball is a tongue-tied kid from Georgia growing up to be an announcer and praising the Lord for showing him the way to Cooperstown. This is a game for America. Still a game for America, this baseball!

Ernie Harwell

Freedom of religion is a principle that is central to our Nation's Declaration of Independence. Congress has taken this positive step to protect our freedom to express allegiance to America's flag and the ideals it represents.

Ron Lewis

After I've been in America for a while, I get homesick for Scotland.

Billy Boyd

The fact that 'Astro Boy' appealed to me as a boy in America was proof that the story and character transcend cultural stereotypes.

Nicolas Cage

Urban America has been redlined. Government has not offered tax incentives for investment, as it has in a dozen foreign markets. Banks have redlined it. Industries have moved out, they've redlined it. Clearly, to break up the redlining process, there must be incentives to green-line with hedges against risk.

Jesse Jackson

It seems to me monstrous that anyone should believe that the jazz rhythm expresses America. Jazz rhythm expresses the primitive savage.

Isadora Duncan

Now we Democrats believe that America is still the country of fair play, that we can come out of a small town or a poor neighborhood and have the same chance as anyone else, and it doesn't matter whether we are black or Hispanic, or disabled or women.

Ann Richards

To drive a car in rural America is freedom. Before I had a car, I'd never seen a rock and roll show, I'd never seen a comic or a show.

Penn Jillette

Whatever I do, it's my business. It's not my job to parent America.

Christina Aguilera

With the chronic obesity in America, it's more important than ever to not only feed kids healthy foods but to teach them how to make healthy choices on their own.

Jennie Garth

Leave America and you'll find that the consumers in many other countries enjoy watching advertising. Not because the products are better, but because the ads are produced to be entertaining. Sometimes they are funny. Sometimes they are dramatic. Sometimes they are just beautiful.

Simon Sinek

A bold reform agenda is our moral obligation. If we make the case effectively and win this November, then we will have the moral authority to enact the kind of fundamental reforms America has not seen since Ronald Reagan's first year.

Paul Ryan

I've never seen America as an imperialist or colonialist or meddling country.

Madeleine Albright

America's a melting pot, all races, cultures, religious choices.

Tiger Woods

When a woman reaches twenty-six in America, she's on the slide. It's downhill all the way from then on. It doesn't give you a tremendous feeling of confidence and well-being.

Lauren Bacall

The most important American addition to the World Experience was the simple surprising fact of America. We have helped prepare mankind for all its later surprises.

Daniel J. Boorstin

Oprah's got good politics, she's got a good heart, and she'll have us all up Jazzercising at six in the morning. This cannot be a bad thing, and reading a book while we're Jazzercising. So America would be better off if Oprah were president.

Michael Moore

America, I've given you all and now I'm nothing.

Allen Ginsberg

I never could get over the fact that The Pixies formed, worked and separated without America taking them to its heart or even recognizing their existence for the most part.

David Bowie

I have no idea where the concept came from that America is an explicitly atheist country. I can't find it in the Constitution, and I don't like it being shoved down my throat.

Ben Stein

When kids can't afford to see it anymore maybe we'll have a whole resurgence of garage bands all over America and this New Wave thing will start to mean something on a grass roots level.

Lester Bangs

When someone died in the wilderness of frontier America, that person's physical remains were buried and the handcarts continued west, but the mourning survivors had hope for their loved one's eternal soul. However, when someone dies spiritually in the wilderness of sin, hope may be replaced by dread and fear for the loved one's eternal welfare.

James E. Faust

Here in America, those who once had no hope will give their kids the chance at a life they always wanted for themselves. Here in America, generations of unfulfilled dreams will finally come to pass.

Marco Rubio

Reagan was all about America, and you talked about it. Obama is, 'We are above that now. We're not just parochial, we're not just chauvinistic, we're not just provincial. We stand for something.' I mean, in a way, Obama's standing above the country, above - above the world. He's sort of God. He's going to bring all different sides together.

Chris Matthews

When I first discovered in the early 1980s the Italian espresso bars in my trip to Italy, the vision was to re-create that for America - a third place that had not existed before. Starbucks re-created that in America in our own image; a place to go other than home or work. We also created an industry that did not exist: specialty coffee.

Howard Schultz

All the sparrows on the rooftops are crying about the fact that the most imperialist nation that is supporting the colonial regime in the colonies is the United States of America.

Nikita Khrushchev

The whole global warming thing is created to destroy America's free enterprise system and our economic stability.

Jerry Falwell

Boxing has become America's tragic theater.

Joyce Carol Oates

In America, there might be better gastronomic destinations than New Orleans, but there is no place more uniquely wonderful.

Anthony Bourdain

America's finest - our men and women in uniform, are a force for good throughout the world, and that is nothing to apologize for.

Sarah Palin

Anyone that has come to America past the age of eighteen will be able to understand when I say that you can never shake your accent.

Martin Yan

We don't need to fundamentally transform America. We need to restore America.

Sarah Palin

When you say things like, 'We have to wipe out the Taliban,' what does that mean? The Taliban is not a fixed number of people. The Taliban is an ideology that has sprung out of a history that, you know, America created anyway.

Arundhati Roy

Ladies and gentlemen, god bless America - land of the free, home of the brave.

Dave Grohl

I'm looking for a deal from one of you TV networks to give Snoop Dogg his own hood TV show where I can find America's hottest hood artists.

Snoop Dogg

Vegas is everything that's right with America. You can do whatever you want, 24 hours a day. They've effectively legalized everything there.

Drew Carey

America, thou half-brother of the world; with something good and bad of every land.

Philip James Bailey

The greatest problem all around the world today, whether in America, Japan, China Russia, India or anywhere else in the world, is that people are not in peace. People want peace.

Prem Rawat

It seems to me the Washington Monument is a symbol of America's power. It has been the symbol of our great nation. We look at the symbol and we say 'this is one nation under God.'

Pat Robertson

In America, the photographer is not simply the person who records the past, but the one who invents it.

Susan Sontag

So this is America. They must be out of their minds.

Ringo Starr

I contend that, in spite of all that might be said about Watergate, Richard Nixon was good for the poor people of

America.

Tony Campolo

Every Teen Challenge ministry is responsible for raising its own finances, but we assist these works with finances, prayer and counseling, especially overseas in areas such as Siberia, Africa, South America.

David Wilkerson

What President Bush did in his doctrine of preemptive strike and in his war in Afghanistan and in Iraq was to turn even his allies in Europe negatively toward America.

Louis Farrakhan

Our veterans accepted the responsibility to defend America and uphold our values when duty called.

Bill Shuster

America doesn't reward people of my age, either in day-to-day life or for their performances.

Meryl Streep

Insisting that we must tax and take and demonize those who have already achieved the American Dream. That may turn out to be a good re-election strategy for President Obama, but is a demoralizing message for America.

Chris Christie

The people of Wisconsin have been good to me. I've tried to live up to their trust. And now I ask those hardworking men and women, and millions like them across America, to join our cause and get this country working again. When Governor Romney asked me to join the ticket, I said, 'Let's get this done' - and that is exactly, what we're going to do.

Paul Ryan

America gains most when individuals have great freedom to pursue personal goals without undue government interference.

Sylvia Earle

America is not just a power, it is a promise. It is not enough for our country to be extraordinary in might; it must be exemplary in meaning.

Nelson Rockefeller

Nobody's ever called me Sir Richard. Occasionally in America, I hear people saying Sir Richard and think there's some Shakespearean play taking place. But nowhere else anyway.

Richard Branson

The liberals think government exists to fix what's wrong with America. They find fault with our Constitution, our economic model and our core values. We disagree with the premise of their argument. We believe there's nothing wrong with America that an extra dose of freedom won't cure.

Rick Perry

Folks, you're the reason that the automobile industry is back. Whether it was the wage freezes, the plant closures, folks, you sacrificed to keep your companies open. Because of your productivity, the combined auto companies have committed to invest another $23 billion in expansion in America.

Joe Biden

When did it something of shame or ridicule to be a self-made man in America?

Glenn Beck

What people need to know is that asthma isn't a minor 'wheeze-disease.' It kills over five thousand people in America every year, and I could've been one of them.

Jackie Joyner-Kersee

My future is full - it is limitless - and my passions for America will remain.

Michele Bachmann

When we talk about justice in America we're really talking about justice brought about by the people, not by judges who are tools of the establishment or prosecutors who are are equally tools of the establishment or the wardens or the police officers.

William Kunstler

When the youth of America gets together, amazing things happen.

Tom Ford

Long live the Unity of Latin America.

Hugo Chavez

If America had been discovered as many times as I have, no one would remember Columbus.

Sean Connery

Do I ever think Gossip will be really massive in America? No, I don't think it'll happen - and that's fine. It's kind of nice because I get to experience everything at once. I get to come home and it not be weird, like in Paris or something. It is nice to be completely anonymous.

Beth Ditto

America's trying to do the best for its veterans.

R. Lee Ermey

In reality, nobody gets successful in America by being lazy.

Bruno Tonioli

I know that I come from mid-20th century America, urban, specifically downtown New York, specifically an Italian-American area, Roman Catholic - that's who I am. And a part of what I know is there's a decency to people who tried to make a living in the kind of world that was around us and also the Skid Row area of the Bowery; it impressed me.

Martin Scorsese

Urban America is like a foreign country in a sense.

Magic Johnson

In America all too few blows are struck into flesh. We kill the spirit here, we are experts at that. We use psychic bullets and kill each other cell by cell.

Norman Mailer

There is no real third party in America. There's this one party that has two sides to it - the Democratic and Republican side. It's one party that has two heads.

Roseanne Barr

It is time for corporate America to become 'the third pillar' of social change in our society, complementing the first two pillars of government and philanthropy. We need the entire private sector to begin committing itself not just to making profits, but to fulfilling higher and larger purposes by contributing to building a better world.

Simon Mainwaring

It is the people who scream the loudest about America and Freedom who see to be the most intolerant for a differing point of view.

Rosanne Cash

In America there is institutional racism that we all inherit and participate in, like breathing the air in this room - and we have to become sensitive to it.

Henry Louis Gates

It is time to let America be America again. To return freedom to the people. To stand on our founding principles and reject the cynical politics of the Nanny State.

Rick Perry

Seriously, in America there are more big, curvy girls than there are little girls, and men love us, too.

Jill Scott

No matter where you go and what you do in America, you turn the tele on and you're confronted with violence.

Steve Irwin

Yes, I would agree that America, just like Spain was in the 17th Century, is the main empire of the world and they are the ones who, on the surface, are the most pushy: pushing their language, pushing their culture - or what there is of it - pushing by force their system on others.

Viggo Mortensen

The job of a leader, the job of a governor, the job of a president, is to get the people in the room and bang enough heads together and rub enough arms and cajole enough to have them put the country and the state's greater interest ahead of their own personal partisan interest. That's what we did in New Jersey and that's the model for America.

Chris Christie

You look at my audience, and it proves what Congress thinks America is, is wrong. I get people across the political spectrum. Parents and kids come and they're all punked out, and there are these other guys in John Deere caps.

Lewis Black

I did very extensive diligence on Al Jazeera English, the network from which Al Jazeera America is going to be derived, and it's really very clear that they have long since established a reputation for excellence and integrity and objectivity.

Al Gore

There's also some element of coming of age during the Reagan administration, which everybody has painted as some glorious time in America, but I remember as being a very, very dark time. There was apocalypse in the air; the punk rock movement made sense.

John Cusack

I firmly believe that we have more latent musical talent in America than there is in any other country. But to dig it out there must be good music throughout the land, a lot of it.

Everyone must hear it, and such a process takes time.

John Philip Sousa

Before the military coup in Chile, we had the idea that
military coups happen in Banana Republics, somewhere in
Central America. It would never happen in Chile. Chile
was such a solid democracy. And when it happened, it had
brutal characteristics.

Isabel Allende

Compared to America or Europe, God isn't a big part of our
lives here. I don't know anyone here who goes to church
when he's had a rough divorce or is going through
depression. We go out into nature instead.

Bjork

America, how can I write a holy litany in your silly mood?

Allen Ginsberg

The Pledge of Allegiance reflects the truth that faith in God
has played a significant role in America since the days of
the founding of our country.

Randy Neugebauer

In America, we believe that competition strengthens us.

Sarah Palin

The challenge for Muslims in America is to respect the fears of ordinary people while resisting the exploitation of those fears by political parties, lobbies and sectors of the media. To meet this challenge, Muslims must reassess their own involvement, behavior and contributions in American society.

Tariq Ramadan

The biggest empty space, the biggest gap in what should be a premier and always vibrant food scene in America is that we don't have hawker centers like they do in Singapore, basically food courts where mom and pop specialists can set up shop in fairly hygienic little stalls all up to health code making one dish they've been doing forever and ever.

Anthony Bourdain

I can't be calm when I drive through sections of Atlanta that look more like Kinshasa, Democratic Republic of Congo, than America.

Cynthia McKinney

Everyone has a right to a university degree in America, even if it's in Hamburger Technology.

Clive James

I felt like the luckiest kid in the world. And I was. I was growing up middle-class in a time when growing up middle-class in America meant there would be jobs for my parents, good schools for me to prepare myself for a career, and, if I worked hard and played by the rules, a chance for me to do anything I wanted.

Al Franken

In November 2000, the Republicans stole from America our most precious right of all: the right to free and fair elections... Now President Bush occupies the White House, but with questionable legitimacy.

Cynthia McKinney

Fascism is a worldwide disease. Its greatest threat to the

United States will come after the war, either via Latin America or within the United States itself.

Henry A. Wallace

I think the most important thing that I think everyone in America must have is belief that wherever they live, whatever station they have in life, that the American dream is alive and well. I think the fracturing of trust and confidence is in the American dream.

Howard Schultz

I love Canada. It makes a nice hat for America. When America runs out of water, it's the first place I'll go.

Ryan Reynolds

I'm not saying this in a condescending kind of way, but it's quite simple: The making of America was a heroic thing. Australia has a much murkier, much more complex view of its history. It's just full of all these open wounds we don't really know what to do with.

Nick Cave

Today in America, we are trying to prepare students for a high tech world of constant change, but we are doing so by putting them through a school system designed in the early 20th Century that has not seen substantial change in 30 years.

Janet Napolitano

Watching President Obama apologize last week for America's arrogance - before a French audience that owes its freedom to the sacrifices of Americans - helped convince me that he has a deep-seated antipathy toward American values and traditions.

Rick Santorum

In America, I'm a foreigner because of my Korean heritage. In Asia, because I was born in America, I'm a foreigner. I'm always a foreigner.

Margaret Cho

All of the guests on 'Faces of America' were deeply moved by what we revealed about their ancestry. We were able to trace the ancestry of Native American writer Louise Erdrich back to 438 A.D. We found that Queen Noor is descended from royalty, and that's before she married King Hussein of Jordan.

Henry Louis Gates

I seek to call America home to those principles that gave us birth.

George McGovern

Communications is the number one major in America today. CNN had 25,000 applicants for five intern jobs this summer.

Larry King

I adore America. It's an extraordinary country. A new country.

Yves Saint Laurent

I love America, it's a much more permissive place.

Amy Winehouse

Right from the first time we went to America in 1968, Led Zeppelin was a word-of-mouth thing. You can't really compare it to how it is today.

Jimmy Page

I'm interested in what it means to be an American. I'm interested in what it means to live in America. I'm interested in the kind of country that we live in and leave our kids. I'm interested in trying to define what that country is.

Bruce Springsteen

I'm convinced that Sanford and Son shows middle-class America a lot of what they need to know.

Redd Foxx

I'm tired and nervous and I'm in America. Here you don't know that you live.

Greta Garbo

This is really America in therapy, people trying to get themselves together and be whole.

David Viscott

The only solution to the violence problem in America is a return to traditional parental involvement. This should be encouraged by every elected official. Also, the abandonment and neglect of children by their parents should have civil consequences.

Bill O'Reilly

The innovative spirit was America's strongest attribute, transforming everything into a brave new world, but there lingered an insecurity about the arts.

Arthur Erickson

My favorite country is America. I love going there! I go in the local lake near where I work on Sundays. It's called Berry Hill.

Tom Felton

In the 1960s, if you introduced a new product to America, 90% of the people who viewed it for the first time believed in the corporate promise. Then 40 years later if you performed the same exercise, less than 10% of the public believed it was true. The fracturing of trust is based on the fact that the consumer has been let down.

Howard Schultz

For all my years in public life, I have believed that America must sail toward the shores of liberty and justice for all. There is no end to that journey, only the next great voyage. We know the future will outlast all of us, but I believe that all of us will live on in the future we make.

Edward Kennedy

Corporate America cannot afford to remain silent or passive about the downward spiral we are undergoing. It cannot turn a blind eye to how difficult the experience of life is for so many of their customers.

Simon Mainwaring

You cannot drive a system that's going to be aiming at preventing illness if everyone is not in it. The whole gaming of health insurance and health care in America is based on that fundamental principle: insure people who aren't sick and you don't have to pay more money on them.

Mehmet Oz

The spirit is at home, if not entirely satisfied, in America.

Allan Bloom

In Latin America, women are supposed to be voluptuous. They don't believe that you have to be skinny to be attractive.

Sofia Vergara

I have nothing to do with racism in America; it was here when I got here.

Paul Mooney

America's veterans deserve the very best health care because they've earned it.

Jim Ramstad

Self-dealing, essentially, occurs when managers run companies to line their own pockets instead of those of the companies' owners. It's been a perennial problem in American capitalism and became a real dilemma when America moved toward a model in which corporations would be run by professional managers who had only small ownership stakes.

James Surowiecki

America's experience, like many others, teaches us that fostering entrepreneurship is not just about crafting the right economic policy or developing the best educated curricula. It's about creating an entire climate in which innovation and ideas flourish.

Joe Biden

The worst, most dangerous person to America is clearly Paula Deen.

Anthony Bourdain

I tell people to look at me and understand that everybody first told me that I couldn't be a 6-foot, 9-inch point guard, and I proved them wrong. Then they told me I couldn't be a businessman and make money in urban America, and I proved them wrong. And they thought I couldn't win all these championships, and I proved them wrong there as well.

Magic Johnson

I have a very personal feeling about how special America is, and I know how precious freedom is. It is a sacred gift, sanctified by those who have lived it and those who have died defending it. My right to speak my mind, to have a voice, to be what some have called 'opinionated,' is a right I deeply and profoundly cherish.

Teresa Heinz

My father described this tall lady who stands in the middle of the New York harbor, holding high a torch to welcome people seeking freedom in America. I instantly fell in love.

Yakov Smirnoff

Every audience has its character; I like America - they love me. I suffer from stage fright, but in America not so much.

Andrea Bocelli

I was a devil in other countries, and I was a little devil in America, too.

Josephine Baker

I had three children while doing a show, as demanding as 'Good Morning America,' so this is - you know, it's almost like I'm less daunted about motherhood, and parenting at this point in time. And I think I'm just much more fit and healthy than I was 20-years-ago.

Joan Lunden

Everything that has happened in my life is because of good government and because the United States of America was the greatest nation on the face of the earth.

Andrew Young

There are some circles in America where it seems to be more socially acceptable to carry a hand-gun than a packet of cigarettes.

Katharine Whitehorn

Something is wrong with America. I wonder sometimes what people are thinking about or if they're thinking at all.

Bob Dole

Most people in America want an easy read. I call it McFiction - books which pass right through you without you even digesting them. I don't mean a book that has two-syllable words. I mean chapters you can read in a toilet break. Happy endings. We are more of a TV culture.

Jodi Picoult

I don't see women and think of them as competition or with judgment. Women really move me. I feel connected to all kinds of women. I am angry because I think we've been mistreated throughout history in different countries, including America. I admire women.

Salma Hayek

I think it's because in America you always get the sense that if you fail, you can just pack up your things and go somewhere else and try again. But in England, it's so geographically small that if somebody succeeds here, it reduces your chances of succeeding.

John Cleese

America has a rap sheet. You can't police the world and tell the world how to act when you're just as bad yourself.

Paul Mooney

As British and French imperialism ebbed following the end of the Second World War, America became the main outside player in Arab affairs.

Stephen Kinzer

Google will be obliged either to accept Chinese regulations or exit the world's largest Internet market, with serious consequences for its long-term global ambitions. This is a metaphor for our times: America's most dynamic company cannot take on the Chinese government - even on an issue like free and open information - and win.

Martin Jacques

I found there's a fairly blatant racism in America that's already there, and I don't think I noticed it when I lived here as a kid. But when I went back to South Africa, and then it's sort of thrust in your face, and then came back here - I just see it everywhere.

Dave Matthews

The way corporate media likes to portray America is as a homogenous whole that high-five's each other at the Super Bowl. But what we have is a grotesque disparity between the rich and poor that is only getting wider.

Tom Morello

Look at music for what it's worth around the world and not just America. In other countries, people are still buying CDs and going to record stores. But in America, it's all about digital. The game is breaking down. But, look at me, you need to know how to play the game the right way.

Snoop Dogg

As slavery died for the greater good of America, and the movement for equality sputtered to life, the white woman was on the cover of every American magazine. She was the dazzling jewel on every movie screen, the glory of every commercial and television show.

Jill Scott

My father passed away a couple of years ago, but he was very old. He was almost a 100 years old. And, you know, he had a very good life. He came to America and he had a good life.

Christopher Walken

Now we understand much more clearly. why people from all over the world want to come to New York and to America. It's called freedom.

Rudy Giuliani

If America is a ship, it looks a lot like it's sinking - financially, morally, spiritually. It's frightening.

Kirk Cameron

The build-up of personal and collective debt in America and Europe should have sent warning signals to anyone familiar with the biblical institutions of the Sabbatical and Jubilee years, created specifically because of the danger of people being trapped by debt.

Jonathan Sacks

I am astonished each time I come to the U.S. by the ignorance of a high percentage of the population, which knows almost nothing about Latin America or about the world. It's quite blind and deaf to anything that may happen outside the frontiers of the U.S.

Eduardo Galeano

Why is it that our young kids all across America can solve the most complex problems in a video game involving executive decision making and analytical thinking, yet we accept the fact that they can't add or read?

Naveen Jain

There is a reason the world always looks to America.

Julia Gillard

If acknowledging that racial misgivings and misunderstandings are still a part of politics and life in America, I plead guilty.

Ron Fournier

The America I know is great - not because government made it great but because ordinary citizens like me, like my father and like you are given the opportunity every day to do extraordinary things.

Mia Love

There are cultural issues everywhere - in Bangladesh, Latin America, Africa, wherever you go. But somehow when we talk about cultural differences, we magnify those differences.

Muhammad Yunus

Because of my parents' love of democracy, we came to America after being driven twice from our home in Czechoslovakia - first by Hitler and then by Stalin.

Madeleine Albright

We have a positive vision of the future founded on the belief that the gap between the promise and reality of America can one day be finally closed. We believe that.

Barbara Jordan

In America, any boy can grow up to become president. Or, if he never grows up, vice president.

Pat Paulsen

Our flag honors those who have fought to protect it, and is a reminder of the sacrifice of our nation's founders and heroes. As the ultimate icon of America's storied history, the Stars and Stripes represents the very best of this nation.

Joe Barton

And fifth, we will champion small businesses, America's engine of job growth. That means reducing taxes on business, not raising them. It means simplifying and modernizing the regulations that hurt small business the most. And it means that we must rein in the skyrocketing cost of healthcare by repealing and replacing Obamacare.

Mitt Romney

I will keep America moving forward, always forward, for a better America, for an endless enduring dream and a thousand Points of Light. This is my mission, and I will complete it.

George H. W. Bush

Alzheimer's, Parkinson's, brain and spinal cord disorders, diabetes, cancer, at least 58 diseases could potentially be cured through stem cell research, diseases that touch every family in America and in the world.

Rosa DeLauro

America is a Nation with a mission - and that mission comes from our most basic beliefs. We have no desire to dominate, no ambitions of empire. Our aim is a democratic peace - a peace founded upon the dignity and rights of every man and woman.

George W. Bush

I have walked into the palaces of kings and queens and into the houses of presidents. And much more. But I could not walk into a hotel in America and get a cup of coffee, and that made me mad.

Josephine Baker

No nation, savage or civilized, save only the United States of America, has confessed its inability to protect its women save by hanging, shooting, and burning alleged offenders.

Ida B. Wells

Here in America we are descended in blood and in spirit from revolutionists and rebels - men and women who dare to dissent from accepted doctrine. As their heirs, may we never confuse honest dissent with disloyal subversion.

Dwight D. Eisenhower

I believe America is the most powerful country in the world and is a country that stands on principle. Its principles are enshrined in its very foundation and constitution, and it has a duty to serve humanity. America has a duty to follow its conscience to reject repression. It must reject oppression. It must reject humiliation.

Abdullah of Saudi Arabia

Imagination has brought mankind through the dark ages to its present state of civilization. Imagination led Columbus to discover America. Imagination led Franklin to discover electricity.

L. Frank Baum

I love America more than any other country in this world, and, exactly for this reason, I insist on the right to criticize her perpetually.

James A. Baldwin

America must not ignore the threat gathering against us. Facing clear evidence of peril, we cannot wait for the final proof, the smoking gun that could come in the form of a mushroom cloud.

George W. Bush

Every day I get up and look through the Forbes list of the richest people in America. If I'm not there, I go to work.

Robert Orben

Some day, following the example of the United States of America, there will be a United States of Europe.

George Washington

Mark Twain was very unhappy with himself for various reasons. He was very unhappy with America of this time. He thought it was terrible we had no anti-lynching laws, and he was also a feminist, and he was also very concerned with anti-Semitism. He was a good man, but he was hard on himself.

Joyce Carol Oates

We regard America and Europe as old friends. We keep old friends, but we make new friends in Japan, India, and China.

Olusegun Obasanjo

The government must give proper weight to both keeping America safe from terrorists and protecting Americans' privacy. But when Americans lack the most basic information about our domestic surveillance programs, they have no way of knowing whether we're getting that balance right. This lack of transparency is a big problem.

Al Franken

It's interesting, as I said on the last tour in America, the audience actually came out, they had to have been the kind of fans who listened to my music via their parents, you know what I mean?

Joe Cocker

Christopher Columbus, as everyone knows, is honored by posterity because he was the last to discover America.

James Joyce

Our teachers at the public school level are the most underpaid for the importance of their job in America.

Dean Smith

In America the President reigns for four years, and Journalism governs forever and ever.

Oscar Wilde

When I was growing up, I don't remember being told that

America was created so that everyone could get rich. I remember being told it was about opportunity and the pursuit of happiness. Not happiness itself, but the pursuit.

Martin Scorsese

Even here in America, people are fighting for civil rights 45 years after the civil rights movement.

Ruben Santiago-Hudson

Freedom does not come without a price. We may sometimes take for granted the many liberties we enjoy in America, but they have all been earned through the ultimate sacrifice paid by so many of the members of our armed forces.

Charlie Dent

It would take six months to get to Mars if you go there slowly, with optimal energy cost. Then it would take eighteen months for the planets to realign. Then it would take six months to get back, though I can see getting the travel time down to three months pretty quickly if America has the will.

Elon Musk

Well, let me tell you, after three years of Obama, we are hopeless and changeless, and we need Mitt Romney to bring us back, to bring America back.

Chris Christie

The challenge to America is to extend to Asia the defensive shield of American power in forms consonant with Asian freedom and self-respect.

Ferdinand Marcos

America glories in its tradition of the self-made individual. Political candidates compete to be a friend to entrepreneurs, and policymakers, imagining the next Microsoft or Google, design laws to back the innovator in the garage.

Mark McKinnon

Greed and globalization aren't just America's fault.

Arlo Guthrie

America I'm putting my queer shoulder to the wheel.

Allen Ginsberg

There's no royalty in America, so people deify actors.

Joseph Gordon-Levitt

There is a deep sadness to American poverty, greater than the sadness of any other kind. It's because America has such an ideology of success.

Will Self

According to USA today, the average length of an attention span of a man in America is 23 minutes.

Robert Fripp

Life, especially in America, is ruled by corporations.

Tommy Chong

I think all in all, one thing a lot of plays seem to be saying is that we need to, as black Americans, to make a connection with our past in order to determine the kind of future we're going to have. In other words, we simply need to know who we are in relation to our historical presence in America.

August Wilson

Successive American presidents have turned a blind eye to piles of evidence that Saudi money is being used to foment holy war against America.

Stephen Kinzer

People on death row, the treatment of animals, women's right to choose. So much in America is based on religious fundamentalist Christianity. Grow up! This is the modern world!

Eddie Vedder

The person who takes the oath of office in the next four months will shape not just the next four years, but the next forty years of our nation. In these next four years, we need proven leadership, proven judgment and proven values. America needs four more years of President Barack Obama.

Rahm Emanuel

When December comes, can 'The Nutcracker' be far behind? No, it can't - not in America, anyway.

Robert Gottlieb

I loved every place I lived and traveled. London, Paris, Rome, Venice. I fell hard for Central America and Mexico. In each country, I had fantasies that I could live there.

Frances Mayes

Color categories are on steroids in Latin America. I find that fascinating. It's very difficult for Americans, particularly African-Americans to understand or sympathize with.

Henry Louis Gates

What I like about playing America is you can be pretty sure you're not going to get hit with a full can of beer when you're singing and I really enjoy that!

Joe Strummer

I think it no accident that most of those emigrating to America in the 19th century identified with the Democratic

Party. We are a heterogeneous party made up of Americans of diverse backgrounds.

Barbara Jordan

It could fairly be said that America, during the Bush years, has entered an Age of Denial - arguably the first stage of a nation's decline.

Graydon Carter

I'm still heard on 1,500 radio stations across North America every day, about 220 million people a day in 150 countries.

James Dobson

The traditional American family has always been the foundation for success in America.

Bill O'Reilly

Materialism has never been so ominous as now in North America, as management takes over.

Arthur Erickson

My mixed-race background made me a broad person, able to relate to different cultures. But any woman of colour, even a mixed colour, is seen as black in America. So that's how I regard myself.

Alicia Keys

And if there's any hope for America, it lies in a revolution, and if there's any hope for a revolution in America, it lies in getting Elvis Presley to become Che Guevara.

Phil Ochs

All the perplexities, confusion and distress in America arise, not from defects in their Constitution or Confederation, not from want of honor or virtue, so much as from the downright ignorance of the nature of coin, credit and circulation.

John Adams

A free America... means just this: individual freedom for all, rich or poor, or else this system of government we call democracy is only an expedient to enslave man to the machine and make him like it.

Frank Lloyd Wright

I also hate those holidays that fall on a Monday where you
don't get mail, those fake holidays like Columbus Day.
What did Christopher Columbus do, discover America? If
he hadn't, somebody else would have and we'd still be here.
Big deal.

John Waters

When we see that our problem is so complicated and so all-
encompassing in its intent and content, then we realize that
it is no longer a Negro problem, confined only to the
American Negro; that it is no longer an American problem,
confined only to America, but it is a problem for humanity.

Malcolm X

If you allow one single germ, one single seed of slavery to
remain in the soil of America... that germ will spring up,
that noxious weed will thrive, and again stifle the growth,
wither the leaves, blast the flowers and poison the fair fruits
of freedom.

Ernestine Rose

You want to buy cars and houses and castles, all of that's on
you and how America has systematized your mind to be

into materialism. Hip-hop ain't got nothing to do with that. I'm glad that anybody making money has picked themselves up - I just want them to give some of it back to the community.

Afrika Bambaataa

And we can celebrate when we have a government that has earned back the trust of the people it serves... when we have a government that honors our Constitution and stands up for the values that have made America, America: economic freedom, individual liberty, and personal responsibility.

John Boehner

We need a foreign policy that distinguishes America's friends from her enemies, and recognizes the true threats that we face.

Sarah Palin

Parents are working more than ever before and unable to monitor what kids are eating at home, and schools are selling astronomical amounts of junk food in order to supplement shrinking budgets. It's a ticking time bomb, and America's children are exploding.

Lisa Ling

This whole thing about reality television to me is really indicative of America saying we're not satisfied just watching television, we want to star in our own TV shows. We want you to discover us and put us in your own TV show, and we want television to be about us, finally.

Steven Spielberg

America is not a blanket woven from one thread, one color, one cloth.

Jesse Jackson

There is no greater country on Earth for entrepreneurship than America. In every category, from the high-tech world of Silicon Valley, where I live, to University R&D labs, to countless Main Street small business owners, Americans are taking risks, embracing new ideas and - most importantly - creating jobs.

Eric Ries

I got my story, my dream, from America. The hero I had is Forrest Gump... I like that guy. I've been watching that movie about 10 times. Every time I get frustrated, I watch the movie. I watched the movie before I came here again to New York. I watched the movie again telling me that no matter whatever changed, you are you.

Jack Ma

America makes prodigious mistakes, America has colossal faults, but one thing cannot be denied: America is always on the move. She may be going to Hell, of course, but at least she isn't standing still.

e. e. cummings

The threat posed by Bank of America isn't just financial - it's a full-blown assault on the American dream. Where's the incentive to play fair and do well, when what we see rewarded at the highest levels of society is failure, stupidity, incompetence and meanness? If this is what winning in our system looks like, who doesn't want to be a loser?

Matt Taibbi

Why don't we hear more about and from Asians when it comes to race in America? Are Asians the new Invisible Man - there but not there? In some ways, yeah. Blacks and whites are always carping about the metrics of racism. And any conversation about immigration reform is immediately flipped into a referendum on Hispanics.

John Ridley

There is nothing wrong with America that faith, love of freedom, intelligence, and energy of her citizens cannot cure.

Dwight D. Eisenhower

Posterity is the world to come; the world for whom we hold our ideals, from whom we have borrowed our planet, and to whom we bear sacred responsibility. We must do what America does best: offer more opportunity to all and demand responsibility from all.

William J. Clinton

Violence is a part of America. I don't want to single out rap music. Let's be honest. America's the most violent country in the history of the world, that's just the way it is. We're all affected by it.

Spike Lee

The fact that we are here today to debate raising America's debt limit is a sign of leadership failure. America has a debt problem and a failure of leadership. Americans deserve better. I, therefore, intend to oppose the effort to increase America's debt.

Barack Obama

This is the basis, and I am not being tried for whether I am a Communist, I am being tried for fighting for the rights of my people, who are still second-class citizens in this United States of America.

Paul Robeson

More than 48 million men and women have served America well and faithfully in military uniform.

Steve Buyer

France, and the whole of Europe have a great culture and an amazing history. Most important thing though is that people there know how to live! In America they've forgotten all about it. I'm afraid that the American culture is a disaster.

Johnny Depp

You grow up in America and you're told from day one, 'This is the land of opportunity.' That everybody has an equal chance to make it in this country. And then you look at places like Harlem, and you say, 'That is absolutely a lie.'

Geoffrey Canada

If you're thinking of coming to America, this is what it's like: you've got your Comfort Inn, you've got your Best Western, and you've got your Red Lobster where you eat. Everybody's very fat, everybody's very stupid and everybody's very rude - it's not a holiday programme, it's the truth.

Jeremy Clarkson

Fairness is not the end result, it's the opportunity. And everybody in America today has the opportunity to get ahead.

Tim Huelskamp

I think America's food culture is embedded in fast-food culture. And the real question that we have is: How are we going to teach slow-food values in a fast-food world? Of course, it's very, very difficult to do, especially when children have grown up eating fast food and the values that go with that.

Alice Waters

When I grew up, in Taiwan, the Korean War was seen as a good war, where America protected Asia. It was sort of an extension of World War II. And it was, of course, the peak of the Cold War. People in Taiwan were generally proAmerican. The Korean War made Japan. And then the Vietnam War made Taiwan. There is some truth to that.

Ang Lee

When you're born you get a ticket to the freak show. When you're born in America, you get a front row seat.

George Carlin

If the United States of America or Britain is having elections, they don't ask for observers from Africa or from Asia. But when we have elections, they want observers.

Nelson Mandela

There are millions of Americans outside Washington who

are tired of stale political arguments and are moving this country forward. They believe, and I believe, that here in America, our success should depend not on accident of birth, but the strength of our work ethic and the scope of our dreams.

Barack Obama

If you paid Americans a living wage, they would be able to pay for products made by Americans in America.

Henry Rollins

I think every chef, not just in America, but across the world, has a double-edged sword - two jackets, one that's driven, a self-confessed perfectionist, thoroughbred, hate incompetence and switch off the stove, take off the jacket and become a family man.

Gordon Ramsay

Today we did what we had to do. They counted on America to be passive. They counted wrong.

Ronald Reagan

Laughter is America's most important export.

Walt Disney

Once you 'got' Pop, you could never see a sign again the same way again. And once you thought Pop, you could never see America the same way again.

Andy Warhol

We do not have a money problem in America. We have a values and priorities problem.

Marian Wright Edelman

Gang violence in America is not a sudden problem. It has been a part of urban life for years, offering an aggressive definition and identity to those seeking a place to belong in the chaos of large metropolitan areas.

Dave Reichert

There are 316 million people in the United States of America. About six million of them watch 'Homeland,' Showtime's thriller about world terror, paranoia, and bipolar disorder. That's about 2 percent of the population;

roughly what the guy with the beard running on the
Libertarian Party ticket gets when he runs for Congress.

Stephen Rodrick

Liberal and conservative have lost their meaning in
America. I represent the distracted center.

Jon Stewart

Community colleges are one of America's great social
inventions a gateway to the future for first time students
looking for an affordable college education, and for mid-
career students looking to get ahead in the workplace.

Barbara Mikulski

Innovation is what America does best. Whether it is the
Apollo Project to the moon, developing the most advanced
defense technologies available, the rise of the Internet or
the latest advancements in biomedical gene therapies, our
nation leads the world in transformative innovations.

Martin Heinrich

Our enemy is not Islam. Islam is not the enemy of America;

Americans are not the enemy of Islam. Our real enemy is extremism and radicalism.

Feisal Abdul Rauf

If I read not amiss, this powerful race will move down upon Mexico, down upon Central and South America, out upon the islands of the sea, over upon Africa and beyond. And can any one doubt that the results of this competition of races will be the 'survival of the fittest?'

Josiah Strong

America wants its respect.

Tupac Shakur

I believe the most solemn duty of the American president is to protect the American people. If America shows uncertainty and weakness in this decade, the world will drift toward tragedy. This will not happen on my watch.

George W. Bush

Hip-hop has done so much for racial relations, and I don't think it's given the proper credit. It has changed America immensely. I'm going to make a very bold statement: Hip-hop has done more than any leader, politician, or anyone to improve race relations.

Jay-Z

If a man like Malcolm X could change and repudiate racism, if I myself and other former Muslims can change, if young whites can change, then there is hope for America.

Eldridge Cleaver

I had to walk away from America, and say goodbye to the biggest part of my career, because I knew otherwise my demons would get the better of me.

George Michael

I think that the path that I took was normal in the American society where young women and men are not trained as to how to make the transition from being a girl to being a woman, from being a boy to being a man. And so I think that most young people in America live by trial and error, and not by parental instruction, community guidance.

Sister Souljah

Intellectually I know that America is no better than any other country; emotionally I know she is better than every other country.

Sinclair Lewis

Every spring, this country will be reminded of the Lady from Texas. As trees bloom and flowers carpet our nation's capital, Lady Bird Johnson will be remembered. Only Lady Bird Johnson could, with her vision of a beautiful America, lay claim to spring as her memorial.

David Mixner

If we don't make earnest moves toward real solutions, then each day we move one day closer to revolution and anarchy in this country. This is the sad, and yet potentially joyous, state of America.

Louis Farrakhan

The rise of African nations concurrent with the spread of the Nation of Islam and the civil rights movement gave black America a burst of pride over and above anything they had had since the decline of the movement of Marcus Garvey.

John Henrik Clarke

When I decide who to vote for as president, I ask myself who will be best for America and for the world. An important component of my answer involves my assessment of the candidate's willingness and ability to protect Israel's security, since I strongly believe that a strong Israel serves the interests of the United States and of world peace.

Alan Dershowitz

When it comes to renewable energy, there's no reason America should settle for second best.

Martin Heinrich

For as long as the power of America's diversity is diminished by acts of discrimination and violence against people just because they are black, Hispanic, Asian, Jewish, Muslim or gay, we still must overcome.

Ron Kind

The jobs crisis has reached a boiling point, which is why we see Occupy Wall Street protestors crying out for an America that lets all of us reach for the American Dream again - a dream that says if you work hard and play by the rules, you can have a good life and retire with dignity.

John Garamendi

I want to say at once that I frankly believe that Irving Berlin is the greatest songwriter that has ever lived.... His songs are exquisite cameos of perfection, and each one of them is as beautiful as its neighbor. Irving Berlin remains, I think, America's Schubert.

George Gershwin

The trouble in America is not that we are making too many mistakes, but that we are making too few.

Phil Knight

Starbucks has stores in America in many, many communities that are governed by many, many different municipalities. Starbucks cannot dictate to a municipality in Cincinnati or Kansas City or Sacramento how or why or when there should be a recycling program.

Howard Schultz

It is not surprising that most Pakistanis do not support

America's bombardment of Afghanistan. The Afghans are neighbours on the brink of starvation and devastated by war. America has shown itself to be untrustworthy, a superpower that uses its values as a scabbard for its sword.

Mohsin Hamid

America was and is the immigrant's dream.

Don DeLillo

We were in the heart of the ghetto in Chicago during the Depression, and every block - it was probably the biggest black ghetto in America - every block also is the spawning ground practically for every gangster, black and white, in America too.

Quincy Jones

Quebec City is the most European of any city in North America; they speak French all the time. There is a part of town called Old Quebec which is really like being in France. The architecture is just gorgeous, food, shopping. I'd say Quebec City is the most beautiful city in North America I've seen.

Sebastian Bach

America is a country of inventors, and the greatest of inventors are the newspaper men.

Alexander Graham Bell

There are five issues that make a fist of a hand that can knock America out cold. They're lack of jobs, obesity, diabetes, homelessness, and lack of good education.

will.i.am

A personal highlight was probably when we got a No. 1 in the U.K. and when the album went to No. 1 in America. The top four that week was us, Adele, Guns N' Roses and Bruce Springsteen. It was ridiculous seeing those names there. Being the first band from the U.K. and Ireland to go to America and debut at No. 1 is just unbelievable.

Niall Horan

America's greatest contribution to the world is its concept of democracy, its concept of freedom, freedom of action, freedom of speech, and freedom of thought.

Benazir Bhutto

Let the workers organize. Let the toilers assemble. Let their crystallized voice proclaim their injustices and demand their privileges. Let all thoughtful citizens sustain them, for the future of Labor is the future of America.

John L. Lewis

I learned a good deal about economics, and about America, from the author of the Reagan tax reforms - the great Jack Kemp. What gave Jack that incredible enthusiasm was his belief in the possibilities of free people, in the power of free enterprise and strong communities to overcome poverty and despair. We need that same optimism right now.

Paul Ryan

Slavery has never been abolished from America's way of thinking.

Nina Simone

Automation and technology would be a great boon if it were creative, if there were more leisure, more opportunity to engage in raising a family, providing guidance to the young, all the stuff we say we need. America will work if we're all in it together. It'll work when there's a shared sense of destiny. It can be done!

Jerry Brown

America is the only country that went from barbarism to decadence without civilization in between.

Oscar Wilde

To make America the greatest is my goal, so I beat the Russian and I beat the Pole. And for the U.S.A. won the medal of gold. The Greeks said, 'You're better than the Cassius of old.'

Muhammad Ali

Be courageous. I have seen many depressions in business. Always America has emerged from these stronger and more prosperous. Be brave as your fathers before you. Have faith! Go forward!

Thomas A. Edison

The men and women of Afghanistan are building a nation that is free, and proud, and fighting terror - and America is honored to be their friend.

George W. Bush

Bananas are great, as I believe them to be the only known
cure for existential dread. Also, Mother Teresa said that in
India, a woman dying in the street will share her banana
with anyone who needs it, whereas in America, people
amass and hoard as many bananas as they can to sell for an
exorbitant profit. So half of them go bad, anyway.

Anne Lamott

Say 'Toronto' or 'Ontario,' and the immediate thought
associations are with a somewhat blander version of North
America: a United States with a welfare regime and a more
polite street etiquette, and the additionally reassuring visage
of Queen Elizabeth on the currency.

Christopher Hitchens

I have a dream that America will pray and God will forgive
us our sins.

Alveda King

All these boundaries - Africa, Asia, Malaysia, America -
are set by men. But you don't have to look at boundaries

when you are looking at a man - at the character of a man. The question is: What do you stand for? Are you a follower, or are you a leader?

Hakeem Olajuwon

The National Guard has served America as both a wartime force and the first military responders in times of domestic crisis. Hundreds of times each year, the nation's governors call upon their Guard troops to respond to fires, floods, hurricanes and other natural disasters.

Russel Honore

Sitting at the table doesn't make you a diner. You must be eating some of what's on that plate. Being here in America doesn't make you an American. Being born here in America doesn't make you an American.

Malcolm X

A quarter of America is a dramatic, tense, violent country, exploding with contradictions, full of brutal, physiological vitality, and that is the America that I have really loved and love. But a good half of it is a country of boredom, emptiness, monotony, brainless production, and brainless consumption, and this is the American inferno.

Italo Calvino

God bless America. God save the Queen. God defend New Zealand and thank Christ for Australia.

Russell Crowe

America, you're sending girls a mixed message. On one hand, you're saying to have positive body image and love who we are; on the other, we're being marketed makeup and clothing that obviously turns us into someone different.

Adora Svitak

We must not confuse dissent with disloyalty. When the loyal opposition dies, I think the soul of America dies with it.

Edward R. Murrow

A man builds a house in England with the expectation of living in it and leaving it to his children; we shed our houses in America as easily as a snail does his shell.

Harriet Beecher Stowe

We beg you to save young America from the blight of race prejudice. Do not bind the children within the narrow circles of your own lives.

Charles Hamilton Houston

The willingness of America's veterans to sacrifice for our country has earned them our lasting gratitude.

Jeff Miller

Had it not been for slavery, the death penalty would have likely been abolished in America. Slavery became a haven for the death penalty.

Angela Davis

After all, when the world looks to America, they look to us because we are the most successful political and economic experiment in human history.

Condoleezza Rice

People can say whatever they want about you without knowing the facts. They can criticize you without even knowing you, and hate you when they don't even know you. All of a sudden, you're, like, the bin Laden of America. Osama bin Laden is the only one who knows exactly what I'm going through.

R. Kelly

America is the only developed nation that has a 2,000-mile border with a developing nation, and the government's refusal to control that border is why there are an estimated 460,000 illegal immigrants in Arizona and why the nation, sensibly insisting on first things first, resists 'comprehensive' immigration reform.

George Will

The concept of God in America is very different than it is in England. Because we see the horrendous outcome of religion as being an American thing, in which the name of God has been hijacked by a gang of psychopaths and bullies and homophobes, and the name of God has been used for their own twisted agendas.

Nick Cave

I'm giving life lessons and tips on how to take care of your emotional heart, because heart disease is the number-one killer in America.

Leeza Gibbons

America cannot continue to lead the family of nations around the world if we suffer the collapse of the family here at home.

Mitt Romney

America is a country founded on guns. It's in our DNA. It's very strange but I feel better having a gun. I really do. I don't feel safe, I don't feel the house is completely safe, if I don't have one hidden somewhere. That's my thinking, right or wrong.

Brad Pitt

America was indebted to immigration for her settlement and prosperity. That part of America which had encouraged them most had advanced most rapidly in population, agriculture and the arts.

James Madison

Coming out as an atheist can cost an academic his or her job in some parts of America, and many choose to keep quiet about their atheism.

Richard Dawkins

You have to love your country like an adult loves somebody, not like a child loves its mommy. And right-wing Republicans tend to love America like a child loves its mommy, where everything Mommy does is okay. But adult love means you're not in denial, and you want the loved one to be the best they can be.

Al Franken

But this is the great danger America faces. That we will cease to be one nation and become instead a collection of interest groups: city against suburb, region against region, individual against individual. Each seeking to satisfy private wants.

Barbara Jordan

We don't want an America that is closed to the world. What we want is a world that is open to America.

George H. W. Bush

America must realize, there are conditions she must accept in Asia. The first is a diversity of Asian cultures, governments, economic and political systems; the second, that to run against the tide of Asian nationalism is worse than impractical - it is also highly dangerous.

Ferdinand Marcos

In fact, I believe that we need better sex education in our own culture, here in America, so that young folk learn about things like venereal disease before they encounter it.

Piers Anthony

When I was a child, I wanted to... go into space! To go to Mars. I wanted to explore and explore and explore. I wanted to go to the Lost World in South America - I was heartbroken to discover there were no dinosaurs; I still don't accept it.

Brian Blessed

Although black and white Americans live, work, and learn together now, there is still injustice in America.

Kathleen Sebelius

There is no place, no country, more compassionate more

generous more accepting and more welcoming than the United States of America.

Arnold Schwarzenegger

The men who have guided the destiny of the United States have found the strength for their tasks by going to their knees. This private unity of public men and their God is an enduring source of reassurance for the people of America.

Lyndon B. Johnson

Anti-Semitism is a noxious weed that should be cut out. It has no place in America.

William Howard Taft

What we can borrow from Ronald Reagan... is that great sense of optimism. He led by building on the strengths of America, not running America down.

Rudy Giuliani

The young patriots now returning from war in Iraq and Afghanistan and other deployments worldwide are joining the ranks of veterans to whom America owes an immense debt of gratitude.

Steve Buyer

During the Cold War, America undertook serious military cuts only once: after the election of Richard Nixon, during the Vietnam War. The result: Vietnam fell to the Communists, the Russians moved into Afghanistan, and American influence around the globe waned dramatically.

Ben Shapiro

Some calamities - the 1929 stock market crash, Pearl Harbor, 9/11 - have come like summer lightning, as bolts from the blue. The looming crisis of America's Ponzi entitlement structure is different. Driven by the demographics of an aging population, its causes, timing and scope are known.

George Will

I developed the concept of the Happy Warrior as a rallying cry for those of us who want to restore America to its great foundational principles: individual freedom, personal responsibility, fiscal restraint, and economic liberty.

Monica Crowley

The abundance of cheap food with low nutritional value in the Western diet has wreaked havoc on our health; in America, one third of children and two thirds of adults are overweight or obese and are more likely to develop diabetes and cardiovascular disease.

Ellen Gustafson

I have an immigrant story. Most people come here for economic reasons, or religious reasons, or racial reasons, or gender reasons, or one of those things. I had a good job in Paris, but America was, and still is, the golden fleece. And I've done very well!

Jacques Pepin

America had often been discovered before Columbus, but it had always been hushed up.

Oscar Wilde

There are many men of principle in both parties in America, but there is no party of principle.

Alexis de Tocqueville

Do all children have some inherent right to live in America if they have done nothing wrong? If not, then why should the children of illegal immigrants have such a right?

Thomas Sowell

People in the United Kingdom and outside the United States share my bemusement with the United States that America doesn't share with itself.

Bill Hicks

I often hear them accuse Israel of Judaizing Jerusalem. That's like accusing America of Americanizing Washington, or the British of Anglicizing London. You know why we're called 'Jews'? Because we come from Judea.

Benjamin Netanyahu

I don't have any authority to talk about the domestic policies of America. But as an outsider, I am mystified by the fact that you are encouraged to buy a gun, but if you use it for the purpose that it is expressly designed for, you get the death penalty. That aspect of America is kind of mystifying.

Nick Cave

What has made America amazing has been the fact that
throughout our history, throughout the more than 200 years
of our history, there have been men and women of courage
who stood up and decided it was more important to look
out for the future of their children and their grandchildren
than their own political futures.

Scott Walker

Part of what makes America strong is our resilience,
tenacity, innovation and our willingness to be optimistic
about our future. I know that President Obama is absolutely
the best president to lead our country in the right direction.

Valerie Jarrett

www.ingramcontent.com/pod-product-compliance
Lightning Source LLC
Chambersburg PA
CBHW070635290526
45790CB00001B/106